IMAGES
of America

South Pasadena's Raymond Hotel

A guest of the hotel has her photograph taken by a stone wall that still exists on Raymond Hill today (appearing exactly as it did when this photograph was taken more than 100 years ago). On a visit to the hilltop today, one can easily imagine—with the help of this photograph—the ghostly image of the famous hotel's seven-story-high structure fading in and out of view, momentarily replacing the two-story 1940s-style apartment buildings there now. Beginning on page 117, see more "then and now" photographs of the original Raymond Hotel grounds. (Courtesy author's collection.)

ON THE COVER: Walter Raymond plays host to a lavish affair with an Asian theme in the Grand Ballroom of his second hotel. (Courtesy John Larson Collection.)

IMAGES
of America

SOUTH PASADENA'S RAYMOND HOTEL

Rick Thomas

ARCADIA
PUBLISHING

ISBN 978-0-7385-5919-3

Published by Arcadia Publishing
Charleston, South Carolina

Printed in the United States of America

Library of Congress Control Number: 2008926392

For all general information contact Arcadia Publishing at:
Telephone 843-853-2070
Fax 843-853-0044
E-mail sales@arcadiapublishing.com
For customer service and orders:
Toll-Free 1-888-313-2665

Visit us on the Internet at www.arcadiapublishing.com

Over 100 years ago, Walter Raymond built a magnificent hotel on a hill—twice. Today he is best remembered for the way he lived and what he gave to others. Mr. Raymond was first and foremost a gentleman of the old school—respectful, hardworking; he never uttered a dirty word (not even to say "darn"). He built a hotel. But he also built something much greater. Walter Raymond was a builder of dreams, for himself and everyone who knew him.

CONTENTS

ACKNOWLEDGMENTS

First, I would like to thank Kirk Myers from the Archives at the Pasadena Museum of History. Kirk has greatly assisted me in my historical research and is my first point of contact when I need to verify historical fact from myth. Kirk has been a welcoming presence at the Pasadena Museum of History for many people for many years.

Special thanks go to John Larson for use of several historical images from his private Raymond Hotel Collection. We both have a strong desire to share historic images from our personal collections with the community. The wonderful photograph of Walter Raymond sitting at a lavish banquet is from John's collection and is the cover image of this book.

I would like to also acknowledge and thank my good friend Mike Lawler and his lovely wife, Pam. They have been such an important influence in making the Historical Society of Crescenta Valley a great success. Pam produces a monthly historical newsletter, and Mike has been instrumental in building monuments to mark important historical sites, as well as conducting monthly meetings and organizing field trips to see local points of interest. For several years, I have enjoyed our weekly Friday lunch trips to see local historical hot spots near where we work. Mike's dedication to his family and community has inspired me over the years, and I am proud to call him my very dear friend.

Again, my thanks go to Glen Duncan and his wife, Pat, who have both been dedicated to our home town of South Pasadena for many years. Their preservation efforts will always be remembered as the single most important influence in our small city's preservation efforts during the 1990s and beyond.

As always, I owe a special gratitude to my daughter Lauren for her wonderful photography in this book and past books. Our common interest in history makes her a real pleasure to work with. If ever someday in the future a time travel machine is built, I would like her to sit in the seat beside me as we go time warping together into the past.

And finally, since this is my last book with Arcadia Publishing, one final thank-you is in order. This one goes to the staff at Arcadia Publishing and the dozens of wonderful people from editing, promotion, and special event support who help to make my books a great success. Jerry Roberts has been a tireless supporter on such projects as *South Pasadena*, *The Arroyo Seco*, *South Pasadena's Ostrich Farm*, and now *South Pasadena's Raymond Hotel*. Thanks, Jerry, for believing in me and my ability to get the job done with high-quality results.

INTRODUCTION

The Raymond was no ordinary resort hotel. The Raymond's legendary story spanned nearly a half century, was equal in stature to the famed Coronado Hotel near San Diego, and gave South Pasadena a sense of pride that still exists today. First built on a hilltop in 1886, it became a landmark hotel that could be seen from almost any location in the San Gabriel Valley.

Walter Raymond invited families from the Midwest and East Coast to spend their winter months with his family at his grand resort hotel in South Pasadena. During his lifetime, thousands of people came, and they fell in love with the Greater Pasadena area. Many of them stayed, not merely to play in paradise. They came to create a better life than the one they knew.

Raymond brought prominent families to the area, many of whom built their winter mansions on Orange Grove Avenue (referred to as "Millionaire's Row") overlooking the Arroyo Seco. The hotel was only open during the winter months and was shut down the rest of the year. Guests would often stay at the hotel for the entire winter season—blocking off several rooms for their family and personal belongings. During their stay, they explored many local area sites and points of interest. From the mountains to the sea, they visited the local orange groves, San Gabriel Mission, Cawston Ostrich Farm, Busch Gardens, Gay's Lion Farm, Mount Lowe Railroad into the Sierra Madre (San Gabriel Mountains today), Catalina Island, and the beach communities from Redondo Beach to Santa Monica.

The Raymond Hotel's hilltop location provided certain advantages over other resort hotels that came later. The Raymond had breathtaking views of the San Gabriel Mountains and expansive property that was first orange groves but which gave way to a golf course when the second hotel was built in 1901 (after the first hotel had succumbed to a fire on Easter Sunday in 1895).

Famous guests visited the hotel, including former U.S. president Theodore Roosevelt, Andrew Carnegie, and Charlie Chaplin (Chaplin drew the biggest crowd of onlookers). A famed race between an early automobile—the Pope-Toledo—and a dirigible piloted by Roy Knabenshue ended at the Raymond. In geological terms, the hill has a natural spring that attracted Native Americans, who built a camp there. An earthquake fault was discovered in later years passing through the Santa Anita Race Track and San Marino to Raymond Hill. The fault is named the Raymond Fault today.

The story of the Raymond Hotel is a grand story. This book is visually stunning given the amount of professional photography that exists from the families of the original guests who once stayed at the Raymond. What makes the Raymond's story so inviting to historians and the public today is the context of its place and time during the formative and defining years of modern American culture. The original hotel depicted better than any built structure of its time the grand opulence of the Victorian age. When the hotel was rebuilt, it became a regional cultural icon again—this time during the age of the great American industrialists and local area Arroyo craftsman movement.

ABOUT THE HOTEL NAMES, ITS LOCATION, AND PHOTOGRAPHS

There were two hotels built on Raymond Hill (formerly Bacon Hill): the first hotel opened in 1886 and was named the Raymond (or Royal Raymond, as the public liked to call it); the second hotel opened in 1901 and was also named the Raymond (or Raymond Hotel). Walter Raymond preferred leaving "hotel" off the title. He felt his resort hotels were a "place" or "destination," so he preferred calling his hotel simply the Raymond. I will use Royal Raymond when referring to the first hotel and the Raymond for the second. Most literature and references in print will say the hotel's location was "Pasadena" or "East Pasadena." This was the popular reference because of the cachet of Pasadena at the time. But make no mistake: the boundary of the hotel property is entirely within the city of South Pasadena. Courtesy lines were provided for all images that are not from my own collection. I have the largest collection of hotel photographs and artifacts from the Raymond hotel resorts in the world, and it is my pleasure to show you a portion of that collection in this book.

Part of the allure of traveling West was the mystique of the many reported discoveries of extraordinary sights found in vast, open, unpopulated landscapes void of recognizable natural vegetation found in the East. The West was a curious blend of oddities such as giant cactus and redwood trees. The sun sets over an endless ocean with deserts that seem to stretch on forever. It was a place where every living thing and object encountered appeared larger than life. When the transcontinental railroad came, the West opened up for a variety of people, who all came for different reasons. Some came to recover from health problems, while others traveled West to escape the harsh winters of the East. The family on mules pictured above posed by this massive balancing rock surely had quite a photograph and story to take back.

One

A Brave New World

Prior to the 1840s, few American whites lived on the Great Plains, creating minimal conflict with the natives of the region. The lands west of the Mississippi were considered the Great American Desert, essentially a "wasteland" of little value. In 1849, when gold was discovered in California, the land was breached by thousands of men abandoning their homes and families, rushing west to stake their claim. The combination of the Homestead Act of 1862 and the expanding American territory resulted in the population of American settlers in the West rising greatly. And finally, when the first transcontinental railroads were built, another flood of opportunity seekers came to the West Coast for a better way of life and to escape the harsh winters elsewhere. (Courtesy California State Library.)

Gen. Nelson A. Miles and his staff view the Native American camp near Pine Ridge, South Dakota, on January 16, 1891. The buffalo provided the Sioux and other Plains Indians with food, shelter, tools, and clothing. The vast hilly landscape of the Great Plains region was once blanketed by a black sea of burly bison. By means of wasteful sport-shooting, whites essentially exterminated the bison. In 1865, the population of American bison was estimated at 15 million. By 1885, their numbers had been reduced to fewer than 1,000. (Courtesy Library of Congress.)

This family of white farmers built their home from the turf surrounding them. The Indian Removal Act of 1830 eliminated all Native American land rights east of the Mississippi River. But as late as the 1860s, Native American–held lands still dominated the West. When a number of pioneers and homesteaders began flooding into the virgin lands of the West, they often found their dreams quickly faded into a life of toil and hardship. Meanwhile, by the 1880s, Native American lands were restricted to individual allotments. More than 90 million acres of tribal land were lost forever. (Courtesy Library of Congress.)

This is "city building" the hard way. Seattle was literally carved out of the hills with the brute force of hydraulic power. Millions of tons of earth were removed by high-powered water hoses, giving birth to its buildings and streets. (Courtesy Library of Congress.)

The double-headed axe and giant saw were the weapons used by an army of small work groups as they descended like locusts, destroying huge swaths of mature forests in the Great Northwest. Or one might view this assault on nature as a divine right to fuel the American destiny expansion of the "wastelands" of the West into a civilized land of opportunity.

Even before reaching the sawmill, lumber was a building material that came in the form of nearly completely intact trees. With only bark and branches removed, tree "logs" became a valuable resource in the construction of cabins, railroad trestles, and storefronts along main streets. (Courtesy San Francisco Museum of Modern Art.)

This real-photo postcard of Rubio Canyon shows the wooden stairs that allowed tourists to climb up to a series of waterfalls for close-up views. Passengers arrived in electric streetcars before transferring to the incline cars at the first stop on the Mount Lowe Railroad line. At night, the wooden boardwalk was lit by Japanese lanterns, transforming the canyon into a fairy tale–like wonderland.

This 1883 etching illustrates one of the great natural wonders of the west, Yosemite Falls.

Another view of California's Yosemite Valley shows a lone man walking with his hiking stick with the magnificence of nature surrounding him.

AMERICA ILLUSTRATED.

THE VALLEY OF THE YELLOWSTONE.

The Lower Falls.

WITHIN the last three years a wonderful portion of the earth's surface, of previously hidden and, indeed, almost unsuspected beauty, has been opened up, by the persevering efforts of a body of explorers, selected from among men of science and adventure. The Yellowstone Region in the Rocky Mountains is described by those who have visited it as superior to all the other wonders of the American continent; and it does, in reality, fulfil the most extravagant of the suppositions to which its concealed marvels gave rise. For more than sixty years, ever since the existence of a lake, which they held to be the source of the Yellowstone River, was established in 1806 by the celebrated explorers Captains Clarke and Lewis, these marvels were vaguely hinted at and surmised. But the mystery is a mystery no longer; and the official records of the government tell us what the brave men saw who penetrated to the valley, on whose south side are the Wind River Mountains, a snow-clad barrier which no white man had ever crossed (prior to the expedition of Captain Jones in 1873, these solitudes were thought impassable); on whose eastern side is the Snowy Mountain Range, and a grand cluster of volcanic peaks; on whose north side are the Gallatin Range and the vast parallel ridges through which the tributaries of the Missouri pass northward.

It was the exceptional difficulties which had to be surmounted before the Yellowstone Basin could be reached, that caused exploring expeditions to neglect it for so long a period. The Valley is walled in, as before stated, by almost impassable mountain ranges. The famous western guide, Bridger, declared that a direct

This 1883 etching of Yellowstone reads, "Within the last three years, a wonderful portion of the earth's surface, of previously hidden and, indeed, almost unsuspected beauty, has been opened up, by the persevering efforts of a body of explorers, selected from among men of science and adventure. The Yellowstone Region in the Rocky Mountains is described by those who have visited it as superior to all of the other American wonders of the American continent."

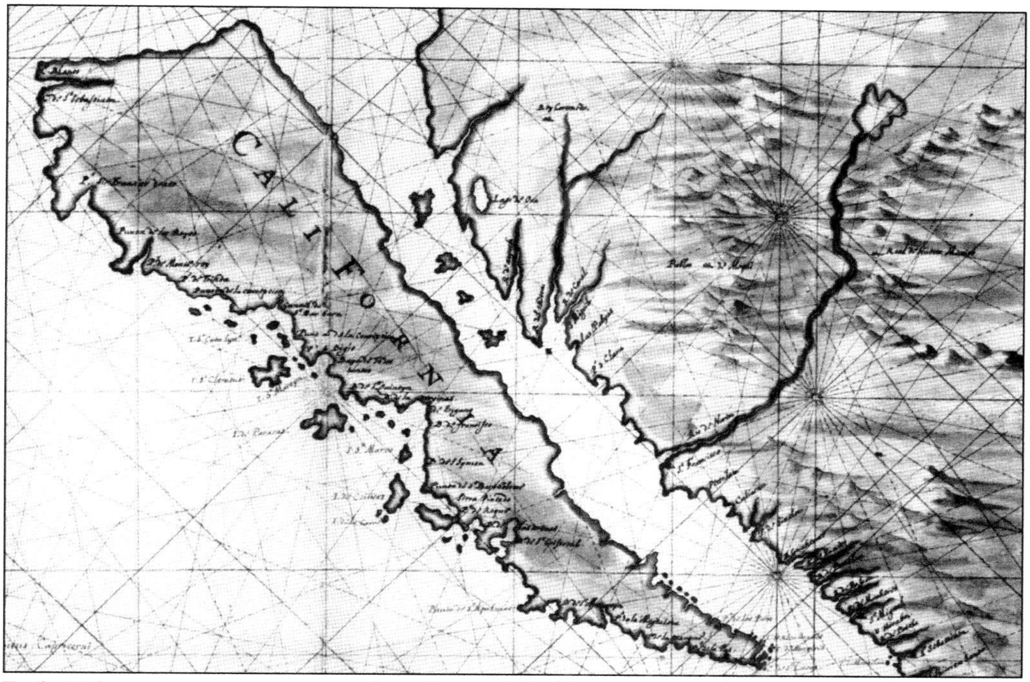

Early-16th-century master mapmakers depicted California as an island. And for the next two centuries, little was known about this sparsely populated land. (Courtesy Library of Congress.)

In the 1840s, the discovery of gold finally put California on the map in a big way. (Courtesy Library of Congress.)

Charles Fletcher Lummis came to Los Angeles in 1884 by walking the distance all the way from Ohio. In the years following his arrival to California, Lummis became a reporter for the *Los Angeles Times*, a *Times* editor, a magazine editor, a writer, a poet, a photographer, the head librarian of Los Angeles Public Library, an advisor to U.S. president Theodore Roosevelt, and an Indian activist. (Courtesy Library of Congress.)

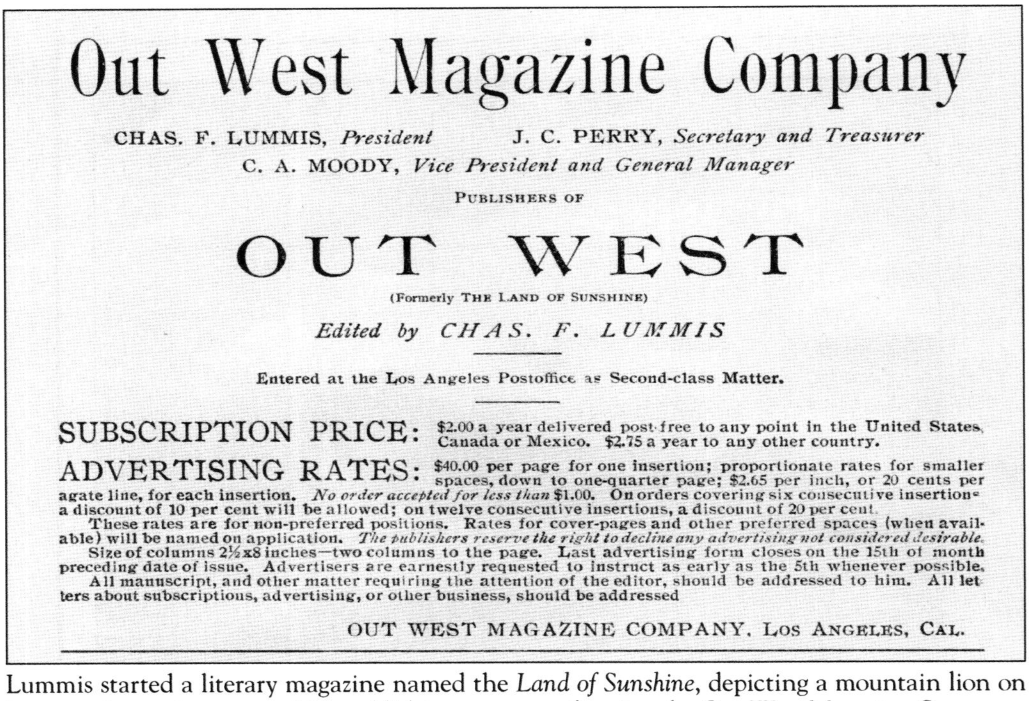

Out West Magazine Company

CHAS. F. LUMMIS, *President* J. C. PERRY, *Secretary and Treasurer*
C. A. MOODY, *Vice President and General Manager*

PUBLISHERS OF

OUT WEST

(Formerly THE LAND OF SUNSHINE)

Edited by CHAS. F. LUMMIS

Entered at the Los Angeles Postoffice as Second-class Matter.

SUBSCRIPTION PRICE: $2.00 a year delivered post-free to any point in the United States, Canada or Mexico. $2.75 a year to any other country.

ADVERTISING RATES: $40.00 per page for one insertion; proportionate rates for smaller spaces, down to one-quarter page; $2.65 per inch, or 20 cents per agate line, for each insertion. *No order accepted for less than* $1.00. On orders covering six consecutive insertions a discount of 10 per cent will be allowed; on twelve consecutive insertions, a discount of 20 per cent.

These rates are for non-preferred positions. Rates for cover-pages and other preferred spaces (when available) will be named on application. *The publishers reserve the right to decline any advertising not considered desirable.*

Size of columns 2½x8 inches—two columns to the page. Last advertising form closes on the 15th of month preceding date of issue. Advertisers are earnestly requested to instruct as early as the 5th whenever possible.

All manuscript, and other matter requiring the attention of the editor, should be addressed to him. All letters about subscriptions, advertising, or other business, should be addressed

OUT WEST MAGAZINE COMPANY, LOS ANGELES, CAL.

Lummis started a literary magazine named the *Land of Sunshine*, depicting a mountain lion on its cover. Lummis revamped his publishing company, forming the Out West Magazine Company, and began selling stories about the West written by local authors.

As stories about the West were published and firsthand accounts were reported back to residents on the East Coast, others began to leave the safety of their homes to travel west. In this satirical cartoon titled "The Sad Parting between Two Old Friends," Thaddeus H. Benton appears beside his motley mule, down on his luck, wearing tattered clothing and torn open shoes. He bids his good friend good-bye as he departs to California, most likely never to see him again. (Courtesy Library of Congress.)

So many people came in such haste that newspapers in the East poked fun at these fanatic opportunity seekers. In this satirical comic, the many crazy flying machines and desperate attempts to travel to California are explored. (Courtesy Library of Congress.)

California experienced several boon enterprises that sparked economic development and population growth. Dairy farmers, cattle ranchers, and fruit growers in Los Angeles sometimes discovered oil on their lands. (Courtesy Library of Congress.)

The invention and development of gasoline-powered combustion engines supplanted steam and electric power plants in automobiles, which further led to increased demands in oil production and improved refinery technology. Large oil companies bought out family lands and promptly squeezed out every drop of liquid black gold in vast oil fields. One such oil field in Long Beach, California, is seen in the photograph above in 1923. (Courtesy Library of Congress.)

Early fruit growers found fertile lands and moderate temperatures in California. These girls are enjoying delicious oranges they gathered from local orange groves in Pasadena. (Courtesy Archives at Pasadena Museum of History.)

Fields of golden poppies and winter sunshine were irresistible magnets that drew millions of tourists to California—many of them returning to become permanent residents of the Golden State.

Tourists purchased large glass plates (known as "lantern slides") for use in lamp-powered projectors for showing pictures of their vacation on screen or against a bare wall. The lantern slides themselves were hand-painted photographs of popular sites found on their vacation. The lantern slide pictured here shows the land mass of nine states fitting into the size of California. Massachusetts had twice the population of California in this 1900 comparison with East Coast states.

This is the original book cover of the novel *Ramona*, written by Helen Hunt Jackson in 1884. Jackson originally wanted to bring to the public's attention the plight of the Native Americans in the missions through the hardships faced by her fictionalized character Ramona. But instead, millions of readers felt the book romanticized the Mexican Colonial life within the California mission system. Tourists poured into California on a quest to see where Ramona lived and where the popular story took place.

San Gabriel (shown in this early view), with the famous mission as the centerpiece of this otherwise sleepy town, was a popular tourist attraction in the late 1800s. It is the only tourist attraction that still exists today. Likewise, the San Gabriel Mountains in the background still appear today as they did to early tourists. (Courtesy Library of Congress.)

The Pacific Electric trolley car stopped at the San Gabriel mission for group tours and souvenir photographs.

The Raymond-Whitcomb Excursions brought a flood of wealthy visitors to the West. Walter Raymond was the first to take advantage of Pasadena's mild winters and paradise-like mix of mountains, fruit orchards, and area tourist attractions. It was not long before Walter Raymond proposed building the area's first resort hotel on a hilltop in South Pasadena.

Two

PASADENA PARADISE

A former resident of Orange Grove Avenue in Pasadena, L. Ron Hubbard (founder of the Church of Scientology) described heaven as "like Busch Gardens in Pasadena." More and more people moved into the area and discovered that the climate was suitable for designing gardens that would flower year-round.

Many new homeowners were amazed at the rapid growth and continuous flowering of the seeds and plants they put into the ground. Vegetable gardens sprang up like magic. Roses seemed to have a mind of their own. Many "Eastern transplants" immediately took root themselves in the sunny San Gabriel Valley and simply let nature take over. The photograph above shows a Victorian farmhouse almost entirely consumed by blooming roses.

This postcard of Busch Gardens in 1909 reads on the reverse side, "We will soon have to turn our faces homeward. But this card expresses my sentiments. California is great. Wish we all could live here. I am feeling better all the time."

This advertisement proclaims Pasadena, California, is "the Winter Paradise of America." The proof of "paradise" is the city's garden-like quality—a place where fruit trees and flower gardens bloom even during winter. "Nature's lavish hand has most richly endowed Pasadena as the 'Garden Spot of the World.' The climate is ideal, the roads wonderful, and the surroundings delightful. Here motoring, golfing, horseback riding, polo, tennis, mountain climbing, yachting, fishing, aeroplaning, and similar out-door sports can be enjoyed every day of the year."

Walter Raymond introduced Prof. C. F. Holder to the area by inviting him to spend the winter season at his new resort hotel. Holder enjoyed his stay so much he promptly built his winter home in Pasadena and became an important community leader. In 1889, Holder addressed his fellow Valley Hunt Club members: "In New York, people are buried in snow. Here our flowers are blooming and our oranges are about to bear. Let's have a festival and tell the world about our paradise." Dr. Francis F. Rowland (pictured above on the horse) agreed with the idea and offered the name "the Battle of the Roses" for the new festival. (Courtesy Archives at Pasadena Museum of History.)

This is how the Arroyo Seco appeared to visitors during the late 1800s. Notice the natural landscape of thick brush and large cactus plants. These early rugged scenes of the San Gabriel Valley region appealed to wealthy tourists from the East. (Courtesy Archives at Pasadena Museum of History.)

Tourists often posed for photographs standing next to a large cactus. The woman in this photograph spent the entire afternoon at Busch Gardens, located in the Arroyo Seco behind Adolphus and Lillie Busch's mansion on Orange Grove Avenue.

Magnificent lone oak trees were never seen before by visitors. Now add to that the mild winters, and before long, wealthy tourists began purchasing land to build their winter mansions along the Arroyo Seco on Grand Avenue and Orange Grove (called "Millionaire's Row" at the time). (Courtesy Archives at Pasadena Museum of History.)

When tourists first arrived at their winter destination, they were not disappointed. The mountains provided a scenic backdrop to almost every view of the valley. Pasadena grew rapidly, becoming a major influence in the region's future transportation and energy interests.

This handsome group looks like it is gathered for an afternoon tea or fine dinner engagement. Actually, they are posing for a group photograph while hiking the trail in the upper Arroyo Seco canyon. The Sierra Madre (known today as the San Gabriel Mountains, or simply the San Gabriels) offered adventure seekers a deep canyon trail, a rambling tree-covered stream, and camps along the way for refreshments and overnight accommodations. (Courtesy Archives at Pasadena Museum of History.)

This 1888 photograph of Devil's Gate shows the Arroyo Seco at its most narrow point. The outcropping of rugged granite cliffs offered shade in the morning and late afternoon, making it a favorite community gathering spot. Local residents would often pack lunches and have family picnics here. The name Devil's Gate was given because the profile of a devil's face can be seen on the cliff at the right (above the two women posing). (Courtesy Archives at Pasadena Museum of History.)

In the above spectacular photograph of Silver Spray Falls in the Arroyo Seco, there are 13 men visible—two of them can hardly be seen at the tiptop of the falls. Every canyon of the San Gabriels seemed to have at least one major waterfall. Thaddeus Lowe boasted that his Rubio Canyon had the most waterfalls of any canyon in the mountain range, and he built elaborate staircases to get up close and personal with each one of them. (Courtesy Archives at Pasadena Museum of History.)

William Lees Judson came to the West as a world-famous portrait artist. Soon after arriving in the Pasadena area, he began painting landscapes. In this photograph, Judson is set up on the Colorado River's edge. (Courtesy Judson Studios.)

Judson visited this part of California in the late 1890s at the invitation of local writer and Pasadena-area booster George Wharton James. Judson immediately took to the mild climate and breathtaking views of the Arroyo Seco and Sierra Madre (San Gabriel Mountains today). In 1897, Judson built the home on the left overlooking the Arroyo Seco at the bridge crossing at Garvanza and South Pasadena. Judson's original home still stands on the street behind the Judson Studios today. Artists of the Arroyo have crafted works of art at this location for more than 110 years. Judson Studios is best known today for its world-renowned stained-glass, faceted-glass, and mosaic designs. (Courtesy Archives at Pasadena Museum of History.)

In 1895, this picturesque view of the Scoville dam, pump house, and bridge gives the feeling of bygone days. The Scoville family built the first major dam here in the Arroyo Seco to provide irrigation for the orange groves of San Rafael and surrounding fruit orchards. This same land would become the site of the Colorado Street Bridge in 1913 and the Pioneer Bridge in 1953. (Courtesy Archives at Pasadena Museum of History.)

In 1882, the Hermosa Vista Hotel overlooked the scenic Arroyo Seco, serving as the first hotel and post office within the future city of South Pasadena. The hotel became a private residence seven years later. The famed astronomer George Ellery Hale lived in the Hermosa Vista for nearly 30 years from 1908 to 1936. Hale was a founder of the California Institute of Technology and was the first director of the Mount Wilson Observatory. Hale enjoyed the views from his observatory in the mountains from his front veranda. (Courtesy Archives at Pasadena Museum of History.)

This 1932 magazine advertisement reads, "Vista del Arroyo hotel and bungalows own a 10 acre garden overlooking the beautiful Arroyo Seco; most scenic natural spectacle in the Southland."

This photograph of the historic Vista del Arroyo hotel was taken recently from the Colorado Street Bridge. When World War II began, the War Department took control of the hotel for use as an army hospital from 1943 to 1949. Today the building serves as the U.S. Court of Appeals. (Courtesy Lauren Thomas.)

Two women are picking chrysanthemums in Central Park adjacent to the Green Hotel. The park still exists today, but the Green Hotel building on the right was demolished. The Castle Green building on the left is owner-occupied and open to the public twice a year.

Former manager of the Royal Raymond, Gen. M. C. Wentworth built this competing hotel in San Marino. The postcard shows the idealized artist's version of the hotel before it was open to the public. Wentworth ran out of money during its construction and went bankrupt about the time it opened for its first season. Henry Huntington eventually purchased the grand hotel, changing the name of the hotel from Wentworth to Huntington.

This fabulous vintage photograph shows the rapidly growing downtown business district of Pasadena during the late 1880s. It also happens to be the day several hundred bicycles paraded down Colorado Boulevard. (Courtesy Archives at Pasadena Museum of History.)

A. C. Vroman opened this bookstore on November 5, 1894, on Colorado Boulevard. The bookstore has been in existence for more than 100 years in Pasadena. Vroman's photography club took thousands of picturesque views of San Gabriel Valley during the late 1800s. (Courtesy Archives at Pasadena Museum of History.)

A

SOUTHERN CALIFORNIA

PARADISE,

(IN THE SUBURBS OF LOS ANGELES.)

BEING A HISTORIC AND DESCRIPTIVE ACCOUNT OF

PASADENA, SAN GABRIEL, SIERRA MADRE, AND LA CAÑADA;

With Important Reference to Los Angeles and All Southern California,

AND CONTAINING MAP AND ILLUSTRATIONS

EDITED AND PUBLISHED BY

R. W. C. FARNSWORTH, PASADENA, CALIFORNIA.

1883.

In 1883, this booklet was produced by local area boosters to make the case that San Gabriel Valley (Pasadena, San Gabriel, Sierra Madre, La Canada) was a virtual "paradise" on Earth. Publications such as this one stirred the interest of such entrepreneurs as Walter Raymond, who owned the Boston-based travel agency Raymond's Vacation Excursions. Raymond scouted the Pasadena area for several years prior to making the decision to invest here.

I KNOW of no disease peculiar to *this section.* There is only a slight indication of malaria, and that probably arises from the frequent upturning of the soil after irrigation, and from the reservoirs, or rather the defective manner in which they are cleansed of vegetable matter. I have never lived in a place where I found fewer traces of malaria. Epidemics do not thrive well here. Cholera infantum is seldom seen, and capillary bronchitis is a rarity cheerfully dispensed with; so it follows that it is the El Dorado for children. Diphtheria is seldom met, and then it is not often fatal. Consumption is a very common complaint here, but *all* imported. Bronchitis might originate here; I do not know. More than half of the adults came here on account of ill health, and yet there is comparatively little sickness, and as far as the weather is concerned there ought to be but little.

Record of the weather for 1879, '80, '81, '82, and '83 to April 1st.

	1879	1880	1881	1882	1883 3mo.
Clear and cold..........	1	9	4	7	16
Clear and warm..........	61	103	85	114	9
Clear and cool	27	27	69	72	10
Cloudy................	30	14	19	20	
Cloudy and cool.........	50	47	57	43	22
Cloudy and warm........	48	29	18	39	19
Cloudy and misty........	4	10	4	10	5
Cloudy and foggy........	31	30	23	7	6
Thick cloudy...........	7	11	1	3	2
Rain all day............	7	9	2	5	3
Rain all night..........	9	10	2	10	4
Rain in the day time.. ..	3		6	6	2
Rain in the night........	1		4	6	3
Showery...	21	20	4	11	12
Foggy morning..........	39	30	26	21	8
Foggy and misty.........		3	22	25	2
Dense fog in the night....	6	4	4	27	4
Wind		2	7	9	2
Hot..................	24	11	41	19	
Sand-storm............	1	2	3	6	2
Frost................		2	5	15	2
Ice....	3	4	2	19	15

In the booklet's section on health and climate, a doctor evaluates the area for known diseases: "More than half of the adults came here on account of ill health, and yet there is comparatively little sickness."

Record of the weather for 1879, '80, '81, '82, and '83 to April 1st.

	1879	1880	1881	1882	1883 3mo.
Clear and cold..........	1	9	4	7	16
Clear and warm..........	61	103	85	114	9
Clear and cool	27	27	69	72	10
Cloudy................	30	14	19	20	
Cloudy and cool.........	50	47	57	43	22
Cloudy and warm........	48	29	18	39	19
Cloudy and misty........	4	10	4	10	5
Cloudy and foggy........	31	30	23	7	6
Thick cloudy...........	7	11	1	3	2
Rain all day............	7	9	2	5	3
Rain all night..........	9	10	2	10	4
Rain in the day time.. ..	3		6	6	2
Rain in the night........	1		4	6	3
Showery...	21	20	4	11	12
Foggy morning..........	39	30	26	21	8
Foggy and misty.........		3	22	25	2
Dense fog in the night....	6	4	4	27	4
Wind		2	7	9	2
Hot..................	24	11	41	19	
Sand-storm............	1	2	3	6	2
Frost................		2	5	15	2
Ice....	3	4	2	19	15

This complete record of weather from 1879 through 1883 shows six different types of "cloudy" conditions. But the number of days the weather was "clear and warm" vastly outnumbers any other weather condition.

Early "crossings" by horse and buggy were especially treacherous when the arroyo was swollen during rainfall. Dirt roads were often maintained at the whim of local property owners. When the trains finally came, land values and population skyrocketed. (Courtesy Archives at Pasadena Museum of History.)

When plans were drawn up to build a railroad into the area that linked with a transcontinental route, Walter Raymond had already purchased land and had plans of his own drawn up to build a major resort hotel here. (Courtesy Archives at Pasadena Museum of History.)

This early steamer in 1885 crossed the Arroyo Seco at the future location of the Cawston Ostrich Farm in South Pasadena. This railroad venture was sold to the Santa Fe Railroad, which operated the region's first transcontinental route across America. The trains brought much-needed building materials and labor to the region. Property values soared as investors poured into Pasadena, making it a prime destination for agriculture interests and tourism. The Metro Gold Line runs the same route through South Pasadena today. (Courtesy Archives at Pasadena Museum of History.)

This photograph shows the full extension of the tracks reaching across the Arroyo Seco from Garvanza to South Pasadena. By the 1920s, South Pasadena had five separate rail track routes crossing the city: electric car tracks on Mission Street and the full length of Fair Oaks, Southern Pacific Railroad, Sante Fe Railroad, and Salt Lake Railroad. (Courtesy Archives at Pasadena Museum of History.)

Three

THE HILL

Emmons Raymond was Walter Raymond's father. While grading the hilltop for the hotel, the discovery of granite required costly blasting operations. With more than 200 workers sitting idle, the fate of the project was in question. Emmons Raymond visited the construction site during a rainstorm, which seemed to punctuate the feeling of doom for the hotel project. At sunrise the next morning, the rain had stopped, and Emmons was greeted by breathtaking views of the mountains and the surrounding grassy hillsides, young orchards, and poppy fields. Emmons gave his son the money he needed to complete the hotel. (Courtesy Archives at Pasadena Museum of History.)

The spillover work crew hastily set up camp on this grassy field at the base of Raymond Hill. With Emmons Raymond giving his son's hotel project a green light, there was much work to be done. The hill needed to be reduced to a level wide enough for the construction of a major resort hotel—to be the largest ever built in San Gabriel Valley at that time. (Courtesy Archives at Pasadena Museum of History.)

Raymond Hill was now a "flat top" and was ready for the foundation work to begin. Notice the nursery operation of trees and shrubs planted in the foreground next to the workshops. (Courtesy Archives at Pasadena Museum of History.)

More than one million bricks were manufactured on-site for the hotel's foundation. (Courtesy Archives at Pasadena Museum of History.)

Workmen posed for this photograph at the Raymond camp after the foundation for the hotel was in place. The entire construction project consisted of several teams of highly skilled workmen. The number of workmen required for each phase varied, swelling up to 250 workmen during the leveling of Raymond Hill and final framing of the hotel itself. (Courtesy Archives at Pasadena Museum of History.)

The building of a major resort hotel required massive amounts of lumber. Fortunately, this natural resource was not in short supply. The lumber operations of the Great Northwest supplied this plentiful building material to the rapidly growing Southern California port cities of Los Angeles (San Pedro) and San Diego. (Courtesy Library of Congress.)

The San Pedro Lumber Company delivers piles of large wood beams and siding for the hotel project. (Courtesy Archives at Pasadena Museum of History.)

The large labor force required to build the hotel culminated with the final frame construction. Difficult to see in this photograph, there are actually 30 workmen posing for this picture. (Courtesy Archives at Pasadena Museum of History.)

An enormous amount of lumber was required for the construction of a resort hotel of this magnitude. (Courtesy Archives at the Pasadena Museum of History.)

Thousands of wooden boards and massive support beams were stacked up high on the graded hilltop. (Courtesy Archives at the Pasadena Museum of History.)

Four

ROYAL RAYMOND
1886 TO 1895

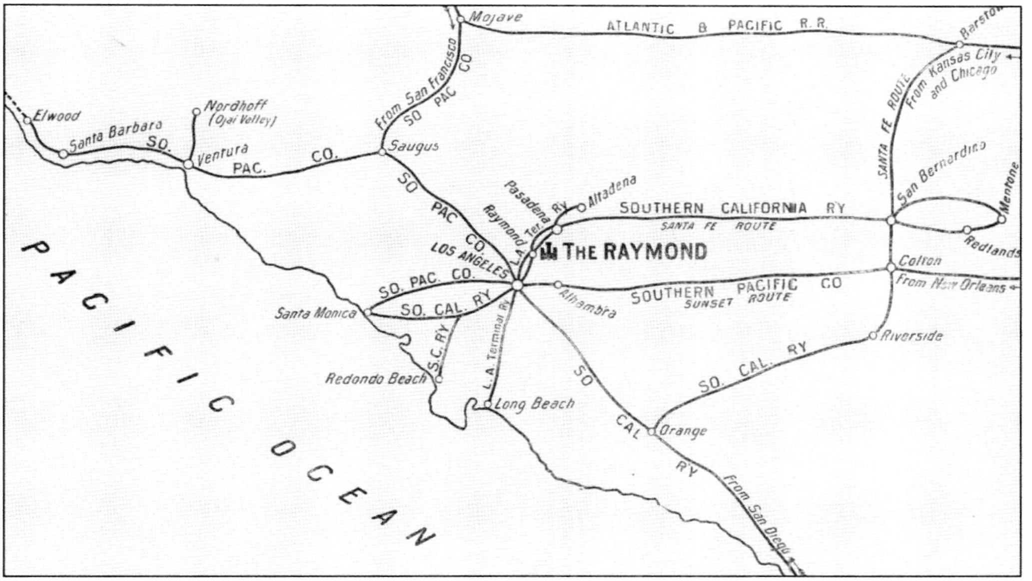

All roads led to the Royal Raymond. All railroads, that is. This map shows the early names of the vital railroad lines that gave access to San Gabriel Valley by bringing tourists to Walter Raymond's resort hotel on a hilltop in South Pasadena. The Southern Pacific Railroad (Sunset Route), Southern California Railroad (Santa Fe Route), L.A. Terminal Railway, and the Atlantic and Pacific Railroad were the original railroads that formed a regional "web" of rail transportation emanating from Los Angeles in the 1880s.

This early etching shows the grand hotel with its flag waving the name Walter Raymond preferred his hotel to be called: The Raymond. Before the landscaping plans had been drawn up, the hotel appears to be sprouting up from a surrounding orange grove and palms. K. Ulrich was contracted to design the landscaping for the Royal Raymond. He was the accomplished landscape gardener who designed and installed the gardens at the Hotel del Monte of Monterey, California.

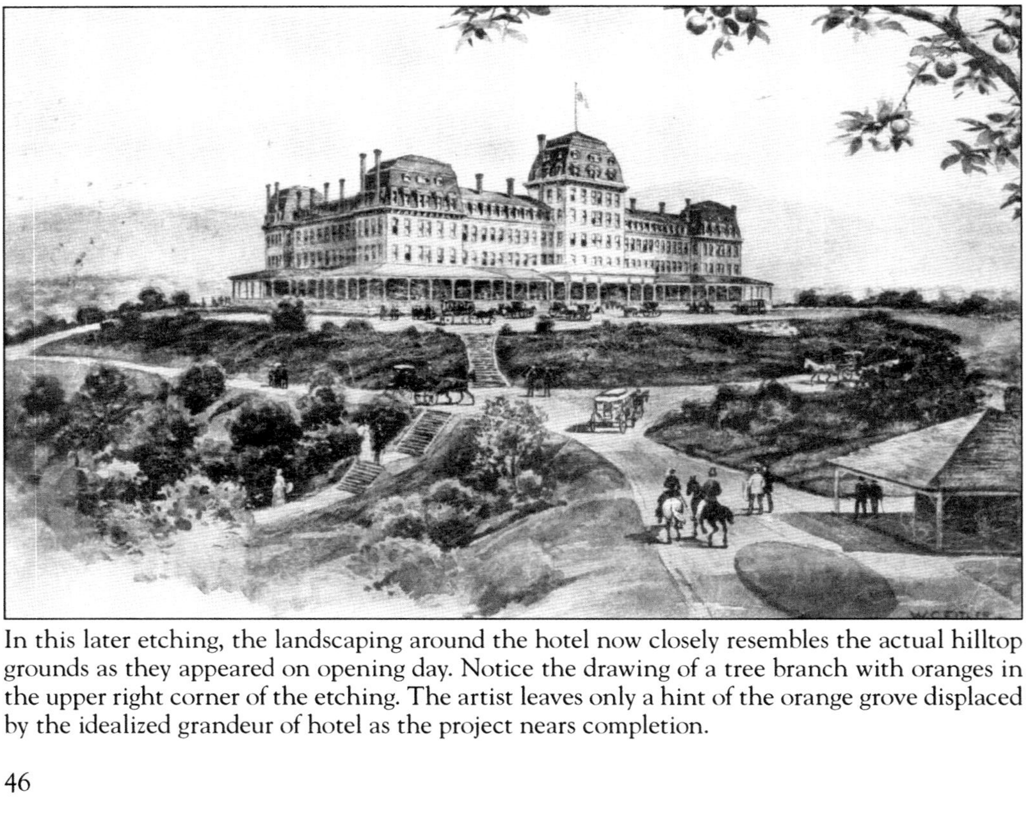

In this later etching, the landscaping around the hotel now closely resembles the actual hilltop grounds as they appeared on opening day. Notice the drawing of a tree branch with oranges in the upper right corner of the etching. The artist leaves only a hint of the orange grove displaced by the idealized grandeur of hotel as the project nears completion.

The Raymond was considered a high-risk venture. A fallen oil lamp or a single glowing ember from one of its two dozen chimneys could render this sizeable investment a total loss in about 30 minutes.

Misses Baldwin

The pleasure of your presence is requested
at the
Grand Dedication Ball
at
The Raymond.
South Pasadena, California.
Wednesday evening, November 17th 1886.

Emmons Raymond. Walter Raymond.
C. H. Merrill.

Please reply

Address, Walter Raymond,
South Pasadena, Los Angeles Co.
California.

This formal invitation was received by the Baldwins ("Lucky" Baldwin and his fourth wife, Lillie C. Bennett, who was 17 years old when Baldwin was 59 years old) to attend the Grand Dedication Ball at the Raymond for Wednesday evening, November 17, 1886.

When the Royal Raymond was about to open to the public for its first winter season in 1886, several advertisements appeared in the major magazine publications of Boston, New York, Philadelphia, and Chicago. The hotel was an impressive wood-framed Victorian building with a stately shingled roof located in sunny Southern California's beautiful San Gabriel Valley, just eight miles from Los Angeles. Travel particulars were made by the established Raymond's Vacation Excursions, which included all traveling expenses.

This photograph of the Royal Raymond was taken soon after grading and construction was complete. The deep-cut erosion visible dates this image to near November 1886, when a rainstorm hit the area, making muddy roads and the swollen Arroyo Seco impassable.

The famed Eastern-style resort hotel was most definitely an impressive sight. Its stately Empire-style all-wood structure had dozens of brick chimney stacks poking up like fingers through its distinctive mansard roof. The main building was 287 feet long, facing the south. In the 1880s, wealthy East Coast visitors stayed at the Royal Raymond in South Pasadena mostly to escape the harsh winter. Some had health problems and came for a warm dry climate to heal or fight off a life-threatening disease.

The cactus garden seen in the foreground of this 1887 photograph was a feature of the Royal Raymond that brought much delight and fascination to the hotel guests. Many of the guests had never seen such a large collection of mature cacti before.

This spectacular photograph was taken in 1885 from the grassy hillside of Monterey Hills. Walter Raymond's 200-room resort hotel literally dominated the San Gabriel Valley. The Royal Raymond could be seen for several miles in all directions and gave its village-like host city of South Pasadena a sense of pride that continues to this day. Monterey Road can be seen running straight across

the photograph in the foreground. The curving railroad tracks running behind the road are along the same right-of-way for the Gold Line light rail through the city of South Pasadena today. In the center right of the photograph is the Center Street School, newly built in 1885.

South Pasadena appears in this 1887 photograph as a sleepy village. One Eastern newspaper reported, "The sick and the well of all lands will gather in this hotel. Weary divines, flying for rest from Eastern pulpits, lawyers and judges, worn out in many halls of justice, orators, lecturers, poets, editors, men and women noted in the forum, on the platform, with the pen, soldiers who have won laurels with the sword, grave senators and wily politicians, all will pace the long halls of this palatial hotel, and gaze from its broad veranda on mountain, small town and the ten thousand bright orchard and vineyard-girt homes."

This photograph was taken in 1888 from the Wynyate (Welsh for vineyard), home of South Pasadena's first mayor Donald M. Graham and his wife, author Margaret Collier. The hedgerow dividing the photograph in the middle marks the border of a lemon grove. Between the hedges is Monterey Road. The prominent Victorian home to the left still stands today, with orange trees planted in the front yard.

In 1886, this photograph was taken from the central tower of the Royal Raymond looking down on the area's young orange groves. Beyond the brick chimneys is Columbia Street, which is the border of Pasadena and South Pasadena (incorporated as a city in 1888). At the upper left of the photograph is the Columbia Hill School; stretching across the top is the Arroyo Seco.

One year later, in 1887, horsecars began operating on Columbia Street, taking guests from the hotel to downtown Pasadena.

This photograph was taken from Pasadena showing the back side of the Royal Raymond. Pepper trees and hedgerows mark this popular dirt road, known as Marengo Avenue today. (Courtesy John Larson Collection.)

The Royal Raymond is seen in the upper right corner of this picture of a South Pasadena family posing at the future site of the South Pasadena Public Library. The woman on the far left is holding a tree branch with oranges and blossoms. Behind her is the Center Street School, built in 1885, which is the location of the South Pasadena Unified School District administration building on El Centro Street today. (Courtesy South Pasadena Public Library.)

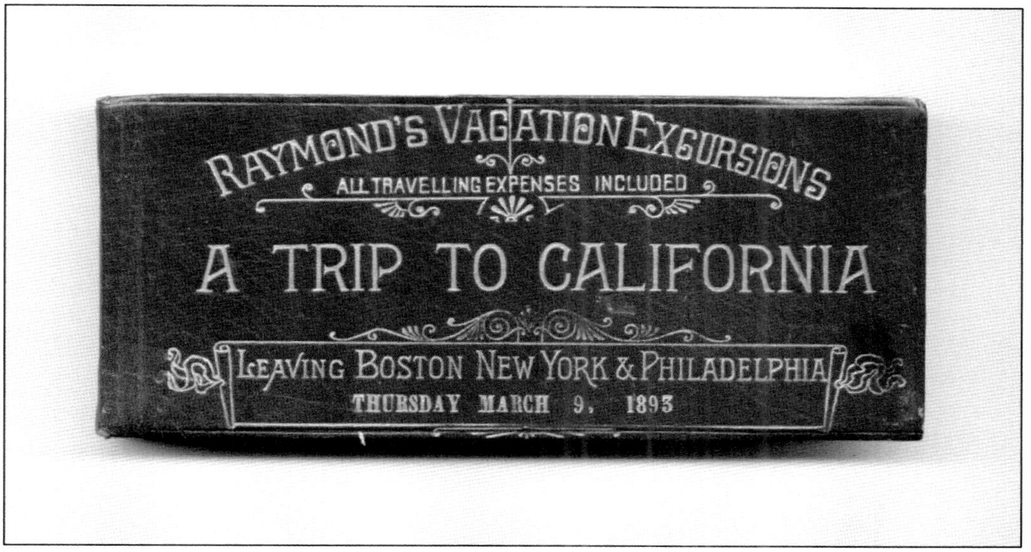

This original ticket book, produced by Raymond's Vacation Excursions, is titled "A Trip to California" and marked "all traveling expenses included." Traveling parties left the three major Northeast cities of Boston, New York, and Philadelphia on Thursday, March 9, 1893.

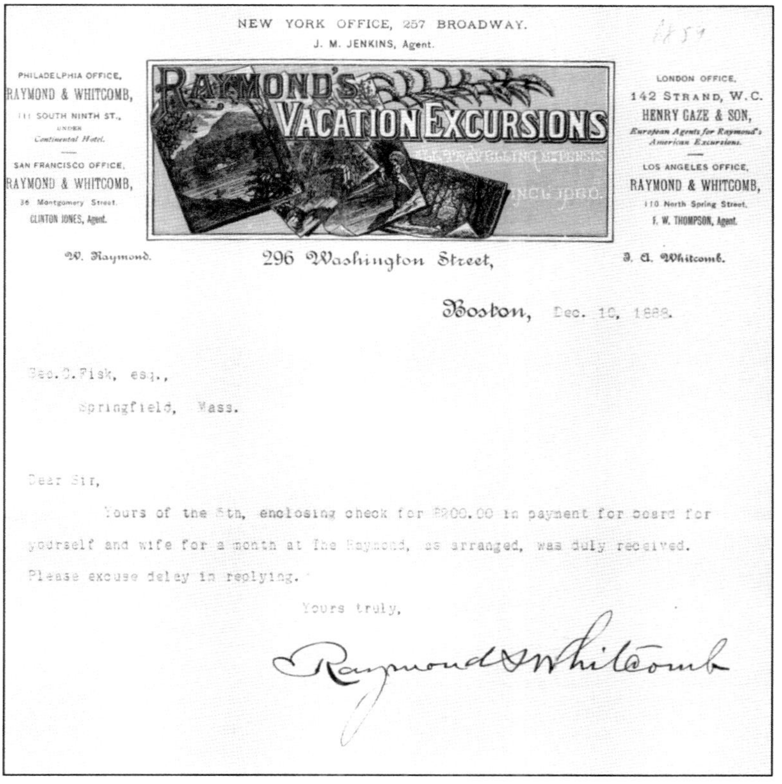

NEW YORK OFFICE, 257 BROADWAY.
J. M. JENKINS, Agent.

PHILADELPHIA OFFICE,
RAYMOND & WHITCOMB,
111 SOUTH NINTH ST.,
UNDER
Continental Hotel.

SAN FRANCISCO OFFICE,
RAYMOND & WHITCOMB,
36 Montgomery Street.
CLINTON JONES, Agent.

RAYMOND'S VACATION EXCURSIONS

LONDON OFFICE,
142 STRAND, W.C.
HENRY GAZE & SON,
European Agents for Raymond's American Excursions.

LOS ANGELES OFFICE,
RAYMOND & WHITCOMB,
110 North Spring Street.
F. W. THOMPSON, Agent.

W. Raymond. 296 Washington Street, I. A. Whitcomb.

Boston, Dec. 10, 1888.

Geo. C. Fisk, esq.,
Springfield, Mass.

Dear Sir,

Yours of the 5th, enclosing check for $200.00 in payment for board for yourself and wife for a month at The Raymond, as arranged, was duly received. Please excuse delay in replying.

Yours truly,

Raymond & Whitcomb

This letter dated December 10, 1888, confirms receipt of a check for $200, which paid for one month's board at the Royal Raymond.

Walter Raymond chose this hilltop to build the first major resort hotel in the San Gabriel Valley. The advantage of this location was its picturesque view of the mountains

The Pasadena Railway Company steamer passes through the cleft of Raymond Hill near present-day Fair Oaks Avenue and Oaklawn Bridge (built in 1906). (Courtesy Archives at Pasadena Museum of History.)

and surrounding vineyards, fruit orchards, and pastoral lands.

The Pasadena Railway Company steamer rests on the tracks for this photograph before pulling into the Raymond Station at the base of Raymond Hill near Fair Oaks Avenue. (Courtesy Archives at Pasadena Museum of History.)

This photograph, taken from Raymond Hill, shows the Raymond Station in the foreground. Notice the railroad tracks disappearing into Pasadena toward the mountains. This same railroad right-of-way is used today by the light-rail Metro Gold Line.

This photograph shows a closer view of the Raymond Station with a steamer resting idle on the tracks. Moving to the right, notice the Raymond horse-drawn taxi and, to its right, a horsecar on the tracks. Other, closer views of the Raymond Santa Fe Station can be seen on page 120. (Courtesy Archives at Pasadena Museum of History.)

In 1892, Walter Raymond welcomes Harvard president Charles W. Eliot to the Royal Raymond. The hotel's manager, General Wentworth (seen in this photograph wearing a tan suit coat), awaits the party on the steps of the grand hotel entrance. (Courtesy Archives at Pasadena Museum of History.)

The main hotel lobby was a popular place for men and women to meet and socialize with other guests. Typically though, several daily activities at the hotel were organized based on gender. The men had restricted rooms for their use only. After all, men were commonly the primary source of wealth and family notoriety during the late Victorian and industrialist society. They frequently gathered to discuss business and politics away from the ladies, "who did not need to be concerned with such matters." Men would regularly meet at the Gent's Billiard Hall for lounging, drinking, smoking, and spitting, while the women would meet at the Ladies' Reading Room or Ladies' Grand Parlor to engage in appropriate conversation and, of course, afternoon tea.

Walter Raymond's entire hotel staff was recruited year after year from the grand resort hotels of the Northeast that were closed for the winter season. Arthur Raymond wrote in his unpublished autobiography, "The guests, mostly New Englanders themselves delighted in the imported ambiance."

While the City of South Pasadena passed an ordinance prohibiting the purchase and consumption of alcohol within city boundaries, the Royal Raymond was the exception to the law.

The opulent grand dining room extended 95 feet in length with a 19-foot-high ceiling. A separate dining room for children was located at the back of the grand dining room behind a closed door next to the kitchen.

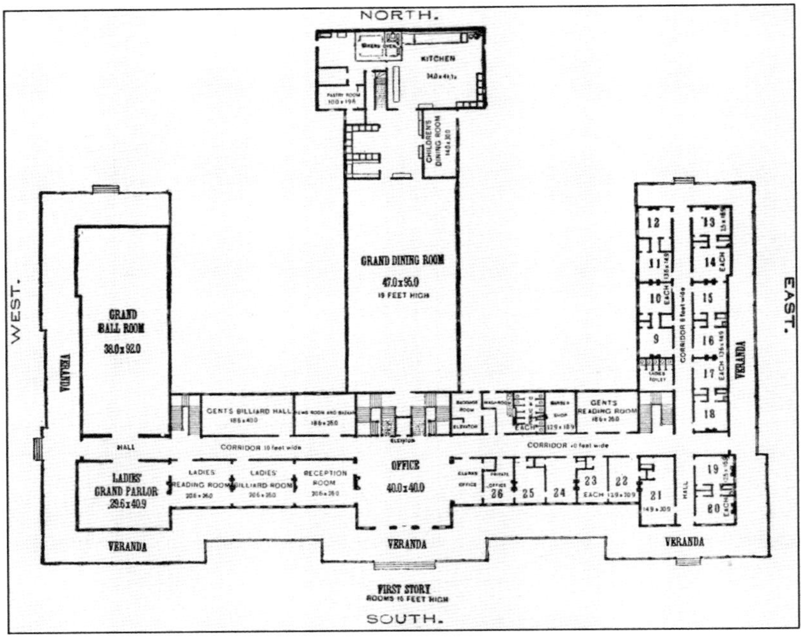

The first-story floor plans of the Royal Raymond show one of the most impressive features of the hotel. In the book *Marvels of Enterprise*, written in 1887, the Royal Raymond veranda is described as follows: "A veranda, fifteen feet wide, extends around nearly the whole structure, affording a continuous promenade of a quarter mile."

There was natural plant cover from hanging plants and front landscaping around the entrance to the Royal Raymond. This section of the hotel's veranda offered a shady retreat for guests who simply wanted to relax in their lounge chairs. (Courtesy Archives at Pasadena Museum of History.)

The verandas on the hotel's side facing the full-length of the San Gabriel Valley was completely exposed for maximum viewing of the spectacular Sierra Madre (known today as the San Gabriel Mountains). Notice the lone empty chair facing a breathtaking view of the valley. (Courtesy Archives at Pasadena Museum of History.)

These dapper gentlemen are hanging out together, leaving the women behind for their afternoon tea. Life on the veranda was many things to many different people: a place to talk about business trends and opportunities, to have a friendly argument over politics, to enjoy a restful snooze, to take a late evening stroll as the mountains turn pink then purple, a lover's kiss.

On the Tournament of Roses Day in 1892, guests begin to gather behind Thaddeus Lowe's personal tallyho at the grand entrance of the Royal Raymond.

This same view about 30 minutes later shows the grand entrance of the hotel as the rose-laden tallyho is about to depart for a splendid ride in the newly formed Tournament of Roses Parade, hosted by the Valley Hunt Club.

This wooden box was the prize for winning a bowling tournament at the Royal Raymond. On the inside lid, an inscription reads, "Won at a Bowling Match at Raymond Hotel Pasadena Cal., Jan. 25th 1893."

For the wife of the bowling tournament winner was a matching designed wooden pincushion with black felt on its circumference for sticking pins into it.

This photograph shows why many of the hotel guests fondly referred to the Raymond hotel as the Royal Raymond. The hotel's elevated appearance on the hill and distinctive Empire-style architecture made it look more like a grand palace in Europe suitable for royalty than a winter resort hotel in Southern California's San Gabriel Valley.

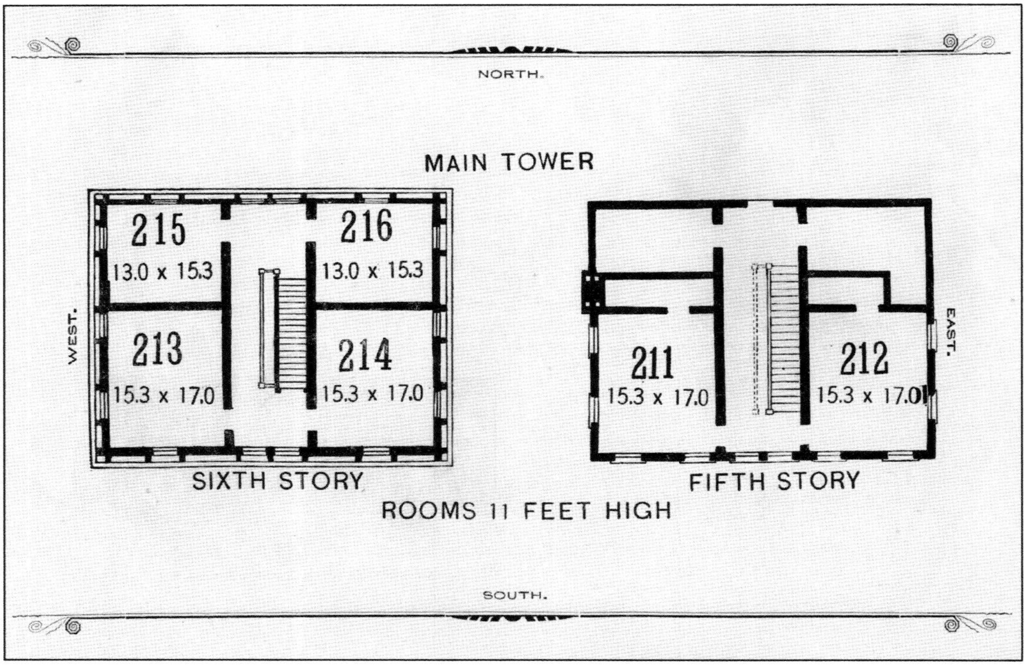

This floor plan of the Royal Raymond shows the Main Tower's fifth and sixth floors. Refer to page 49, top, to see the exterior of the Main Tower. Notice that the only sixth floor in the hotel is located here. The two south facing rooms measure 15-by-17 feet with 11-foot-high ceilings. Now refer to page 53, top, for a view of the local orange groves and Columbia Street taken from room 213 on the sixth floor.

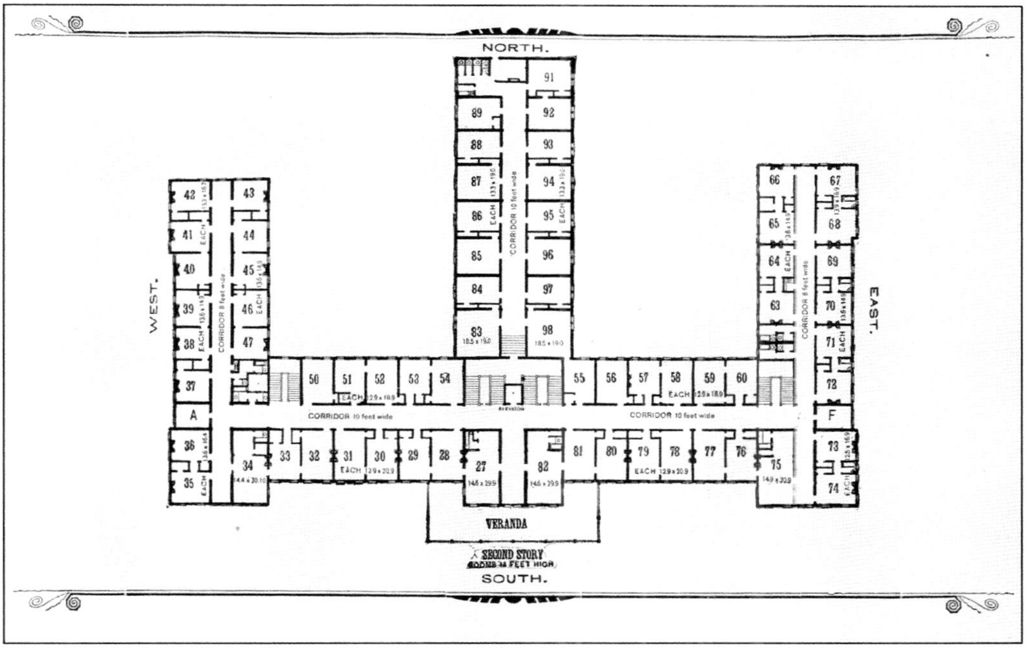

This second-story floor plan of the Royal Raymond shows the Main Tower rooms 27 and 82 with a private veranda, toilet, and bath. Notice also the row of rooms 83–98 behind the Main Tower. They are located on the floor above the Grand Dining Room.

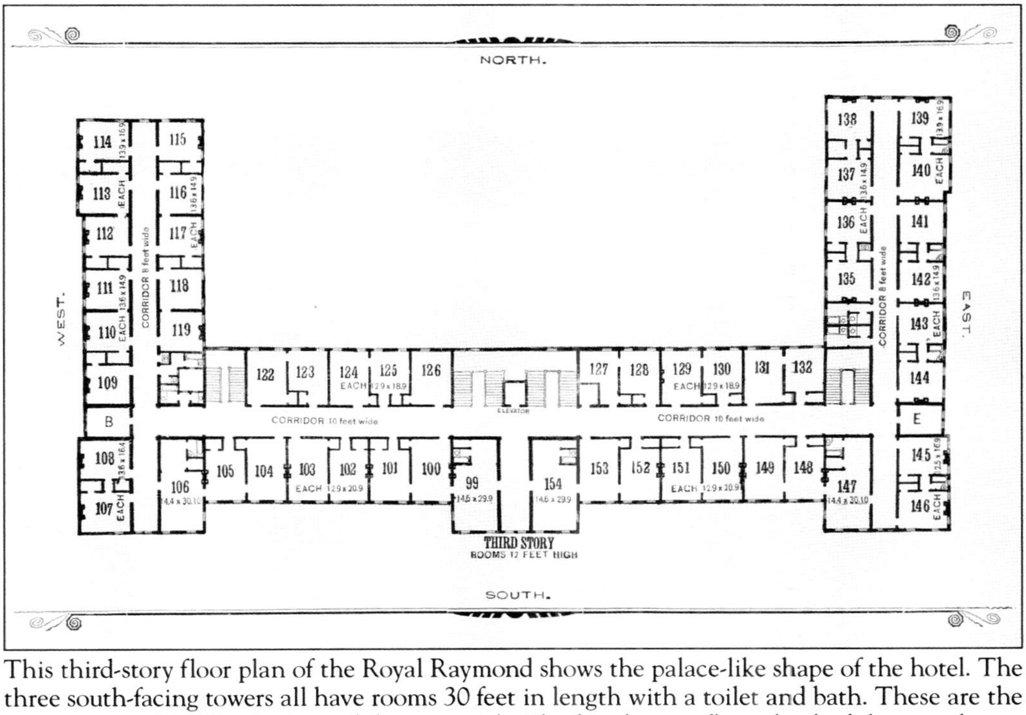

This third-story floor plan of the Royal Raymond shows the palace-like shape of the hotel. The three south-facing towers all have rooms 30 feet in length with a toilet and bath. These are the rooms reserved for dignitaries and the super rich. The fourth-story floor plan had the same layout and number of rooms.

The Boston-based travel agency Raymond and Whitcomb and local area boosters hyped this part of the San Gabriel Valley as a "paradise on Earth." When visitors first arrived at their winter destination, they were not disappointed. The quaint nearby Raymond Station, citrus groves, farm

The diversity of scenery that existed in San Gabriel Valley during the late 1800s is obvious in this photograph. Here one sees a strictly pastoral landscape void of citrus groves or man-made structures of any kind. (Courtesy Archives at Pasadena Museum of History.)

houses, village-like city in the distance, and mountains provided a scenic backdrop to almost every view of the valley.

Within a short distance of pastoral lands are the early stages of the rapidly growing city of Pasadena. This is a photograph of the Lowe Opera House, built by Prof. Thaddeus Lowe, the famed Civil War balloonist and builder of the Mount Lowe Railroad. Walter Raymond's wife, Hattie, sang here in the light opera *Erminie* and *Princess Bonnie*. She was a soprano soloist with the Los Angeles Symphony and frequently sang at the hotel, much to the delight of the guests. (Courtesy Archives at Pasadena Museum of History.)

These Raymond mules were the primary transportation "vehicle" on short trips to town or to visit the orange fields. Bicycles were gaining popularity, but the roads were not suited for traveling any distance. Automobiles had not been invented yet. Horsecars were confined to the rails on established roads. Walking had its drawbacks as well; after all, the hotel was built on a hill. So, regarding the mules . . . it beat sharing a carriage ride with a stranger.

Guests of the Royal Raymond hold branches of oranges and blossoms while posing on mules from the hotel for a professional photographer from the Jarvis Studios. Faintly seen in the photograph is the washed-out image of the hotel just to the left of the large orange tree behind the party on the right.

In this photograph, it appears the women get the mules and the men get to walk. No matter: the men get to vote and the women do not. (Courtesy South Pasadena Public Library.)

This photograph was taken by an amateur photographer showing the approach road up to the hilltop entrance of the hotel from Fair Oaks Avenue. Notice the wooden walkway with a single handrail leading up the hill to the left. If you did not know this was merely the side view of the hotel, you would probably swear it was the front entrance of the hotel. The Royal Raymond was an impressive architectural building from nearly every angle. (Courtesy Archives at Pasadena Museum of History.)

Several aging Civil War veterans visited the San Gabriel Valley in search of new opportunity. They often stayed at the Royal Raymond as the honored guests of a grateful benefactor or Walter Raymond himself. Gen. William Tecumseh Sherman visited the Royal Raymond and summed up his experience: "It is the loveliest spot of earth I have ever visited." Even though this panoramic image of the hilltop hotel is severely damaged, the magnificent Royal Raymond can be seen in all its splendor, positioned perfectly above the orange grove and grassy, expansive lawn.

The young orange groves of South Pasadena were fair game for a professional photographer's camera lens (this image was taken from a stereograph photograph), so long as the Goliath-like Royal Raymond was in the background of the photograph.

This rare view of the Royal Raymond was taken from Civil War general George Stoneman's 400-acre estate, Los Robles ("The Oaks"). General Stoneman became the 15th governor of California. Today California Registered Historical Landmark No. 669 marks the historic site of his estate home, once located near the present-day street address of 1912 Montrobles Place.

This booklet marked Raymond's Vacation Excursions' 13th season of winter trips to California in 1894–1895. The party that left New York for California on March 7, 1895, would be the last party to visit the Royal Raymond.

The Pasadena City Band poses with hotel guests holding small bouquets of flowers. The Royal Raymond sponsored the band and an orchestra during the winter and spring months while the hotel was open. (Courtesy Archives at Pasadena Museum of History.)

The Royal Raymond bellmen and porters pose for this classic photograph standing in the tall grass with the Raymond taxi parked behind them on Fair Oaks Avenue. The Royal Raymond looms over the hill's rise.

Five

EASTER SUNDAY 1895

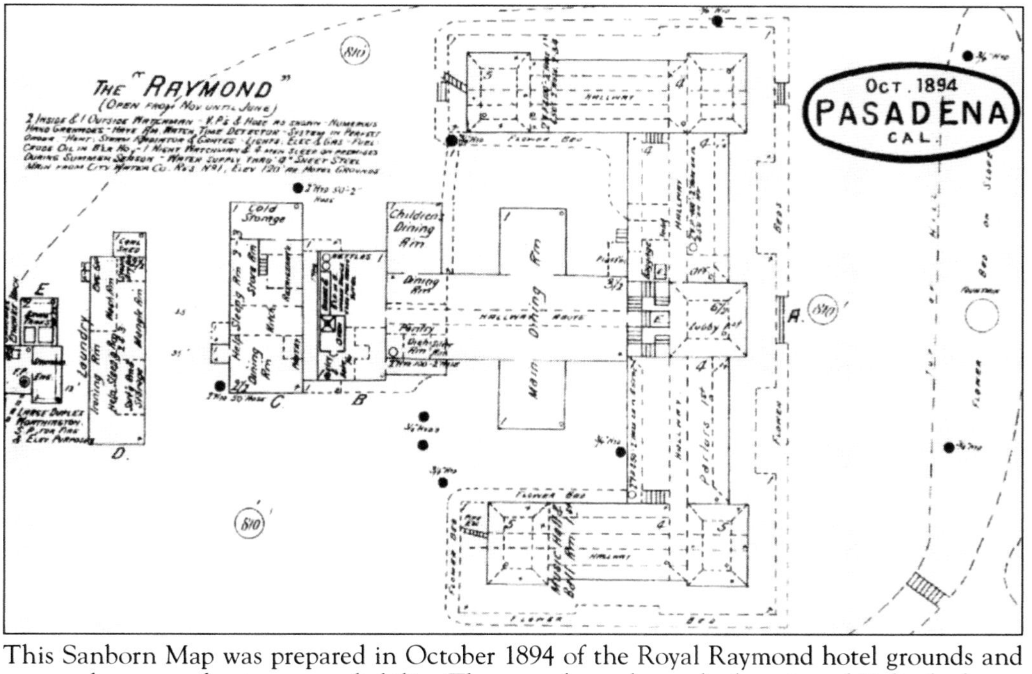

This Sanborn Map was prepared in October 1894 of the Royal Raymond hotel grounds and was used to assess fire insurance liability. The map above shows the location of 11 fire hydrants with hoses that were 50 feet in length. The hotel also had watchmen making regular rounds, two inside and one outside. Ironically, within a few months of this map's creation, it would be rendered useless.

This magnificent photograph of the Royal Raymond shows the beauty of its position on the hilltop in perfect harmony with its natural setting. The hotel seems to have an almost storybook quality, easily becoming a painted scene from some far-off mythical land where legends are born and happy endings come true. (Courtesy Archives at the Pasadena Museum of History.)

Here is a photograph of the Royal Raymond taken from nearly the same angle as the previous image less than two weeks later. (Courtesy Archives at the Pasadena Museum of History.)

The "spark" that ignited the hotel was a glowing ember from one of the two dozen chimneys. The enormous amount of lumber used to build the hotel was now the fuel that unleashed a hellfire of flames and wind unmatched to this day. Fortunately, there was no loss of life. (Courtesy Archives at the Pasadena Museum of History.)

This photograph was taken on Easter Sunday in 1895 by A. C. Vroman coming from the Arroyo Seco with camera equipment in his carriage. He pulled his carriage alongside Columbia Street in South Pasadena and began taking the first in a series of spectacular photographs. In this photograph, smoke can be seen engulfing the hotel. (Courtesy Archives at the Pasadena Museum of History.)

The newly outfitted Pasadena Fire Department was woefully ill equipped to battle the intense, all-consuming blaze of the Royal Raymond. Pasadena's modern fire department had the best equipment and trained full-time firefighters in San Gabriel Valley, but in the end, it was no match for the greatest single-structure fire in its history. (Courtesy Archives at Pasadena Museum of History.)

A closer view shows guests standing with their belongings gazing at the enormous fire. The day was Easter Sunday in 1895—the day of the greatest single-structure fire in San Gabriel Valley's history. (Courtesy California Historical Society.)

The devastation was total. Only a couple of chimneys were left standing. Ironically, the spark that ignited the Royal Raymond was a glowing ember from one of the two dozen chimneys. Now these blackened chimneys stand as eerie reminders of the cause of the devastation. (Courtesy South Pasadena Public Library.)

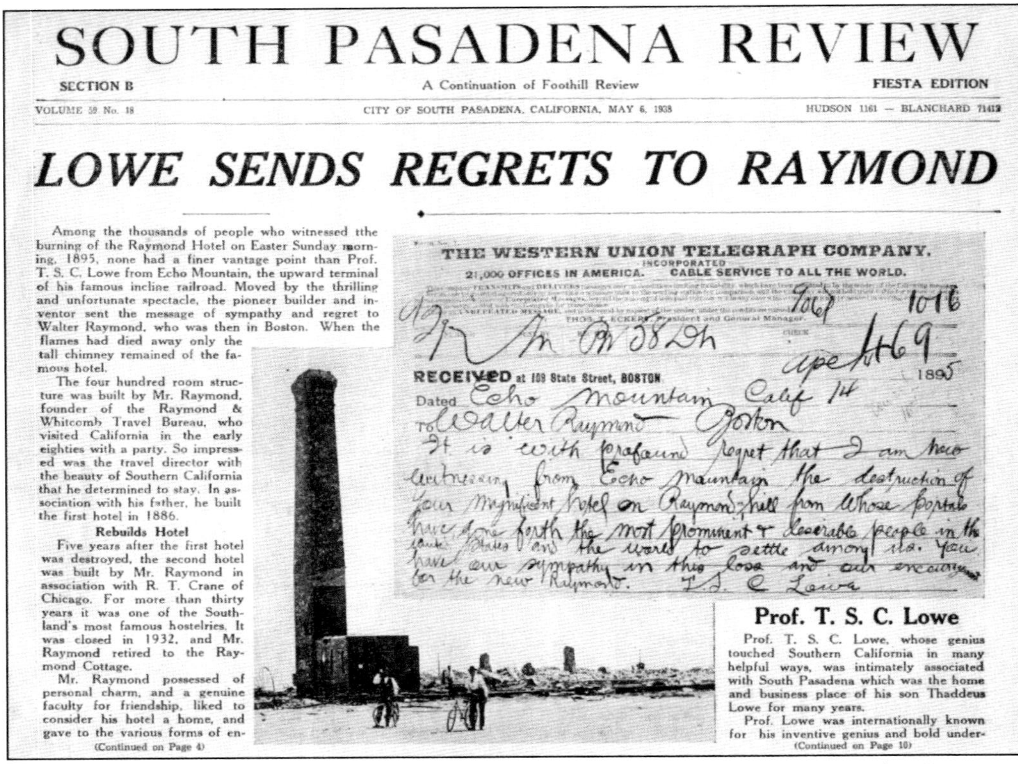

SOUTH PASADENA REVIEW

SECTION B — A Continuation of Foothill Review — FIESTA EDITION

VOLUME 59 No. 18 — CITY OF SOUTH PASADENA, CALIFORNIA, MAY 6, 1938 — HUDSON 1161 — BLANCHARD 71412

LOWE SENDS REGRETS TO RAYMOND

Among the thousands of people who witnessed tthe burning of the Raymond Hotel on Easter Sunday morning, 1895, none had a finer vantage point than Prof. T. S. C. Lowe from Echo Mountain, the upward terminal of his famous incline railroad. Moved by the thrilling and unfortunate spectacle, the pioneer builder and inventor sent the message of sympathy and regret to Walter Raymond, who was then in Boston. When the flames had died away only the tall chimney remained of the famous hotel.

The four hundred room structure was built by Mr. Raymond, founder of the Raymond & Whitcomb Travel Bureau, who visited California in the early eighties with a party. So impressed was the travel director with the beauty of Southern California that he determined to stay. In association with his father, he built the first hotel in 1886.

Rebuilds Hotel

Five years after the first hotel was destroyed, the second hotel was built by Mr. Raymond in association with R. T. Crane of Chicago. For more than thirty years it was one of the Southland's most famous hostelries. It was closed in 1932, and Mr. Raymond retired to the Raymond Cottage.

Mr. Raymond possessed of personal charm, and a genuine faculty for friendship, liked to consider his hotel a home, and gave to the various forms of en-

(Continued on Page 4)

THE WESTERN UNION TELEGRAPH COMPANY.
INCORPORATED
21,000 OFFICES IN AMERICA. CABLE SERVICE TO ALL THE WORLD.

THOS. T. ECKERT, President and General Manager.

RECEIVED at 109 State Street, BOSTON — Apr 14 1895

Dated Echo Mountain Calif 14

To Walter Raymond Boston

It is with profound regret that I am now witnessing from Echo mountain the destruction of your magnificent hotel on Raymond hill from whose portals have gone forth the most prominent & desirable people in the United States and the world to settle among us. You have our sympathy in this loss and our encouragement for the new Raymond. T. S. C. Lowe

Prof. T. S. C. Lowe

Prof. T. S. C. Lowe, whose genius touched Southern California in many helpful ways, was intimately associated with South Pasadena which was the home and business place of his son Thaddeus Lowe for many years.

Prof. Lowe was internationally known for his inventive genius and bold under-

(Continued on Page 10)

The *South Pasadena Review* reprinted the telegram sent by Thaddeus Lowe to Walter Raymond from his vantage point on Echo Mountain expressing Lowe's "profound regret" at witnessing the burning of Raymond's magnificent hotel. Property loss was staggering for the wealthier guests. They brought many comforts of home in their Pullman Palace railcars and often reserved a block of rooms. But, in the end, the guests of the Royal Raymond were men of means who could easily recover their uninsured loss.

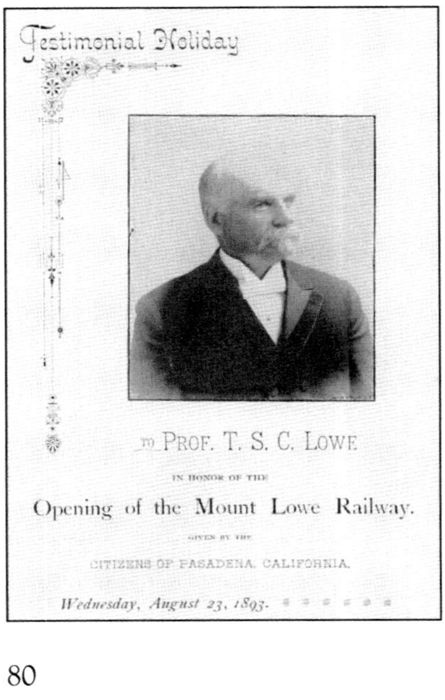

This original pamphlet was printed for the Holiday Testimonial on August 23, 1893, hosted by the citizens of Pasadena to honor Thaddeus Lowe for building his famed Mount Lowe Railroad in the local mountains. In less than two years from this day, the Royal Raymond was destroyed.

Six years after Thaddeus Lowe sent his regret to Walter Raymond after witnessing the burning of the Royal Raymond, he received a note of regret himself from his good friend Walter Raymond after the burning of Lowe's Echo Mountain House (pictured above).

This view, with Raymond Hill in the background, was taken shortly after the devastating fire of 1895. Notice that the city of South Pasadena has become a major, thriving citrus-growing community.

Walter Raymond recovered some insurance money from the fire but not enough to rebuild the hotel. Undaunted, he built this pavilion over the site of the Royal Raymond and invited the public to enjoy the famous hilltop views and share his dream of rebuilding the hotel. The hilltop had again become a community meeting place where dancing, food, and drink were again plentiful. Raymond would not easily give up his dream. (Courtesy Archives at the Pasadena Museum of History.)

Six

THE RAYMOND
1901 TO 1933

The artist's rendering of the proposed second hotel is seen here. The structure would occupy the same site as the original hotel on Raymond Hill. Walter Raymond's son Arthur remembered years later, "It took my father five years to raise enough money above the proceeds of insurance to rebuild. A wealthy plumbing equipment manufacturer from Chicago, R. T. Crane (Crane Plumbing today), who had been a guest at the first Raymond, finally lent him $300,000 to make a new hotel possible."

When the new hotel was completed, Walter Raymond once again asserted his claim to have providence over the best location for a hotel anywhere in America. He often repeated the claim that the Raymond "was conceded by exacting critics to be the most superbly located hotel on the American content, with every appointment perfect."

Arthur Raymond wrote in his unpublished autobiography (1974) that his father, Walter, gave a "little speech" during opening day of his new hotel: "When great ships are launched upon the ocean a beautiful young lady performs the ceremony, but in opening this hotel to the public I shall have it done by my little boy three years of age, Master Arthur Emmons Raymond."

This newspaper advertisement reads, "The Raymond is the winter home of persons who want the best—its location is the best in the world. Raymond Park in which it is located, comprises seventy-five acres, and has within its borders a nine-hole Golf Course, that cannot be surpassed for attractiveness of scenery, or for all the fine points that appeal to lovers of the game. The course is green throughout the winter months, and there's nothing more exhilarating than a game on its grassy slopes."

WALTER RAYMOND Proprietor | THE RAYMOND | M. C. WENTWORTH Manager

THE FINEST LOCATED HOTEL IN THE WORLD—A PLACE FOR PARTICULAR PEOPLE

The Raymond is the winter home of persons who want the best—its location is the best in the world, and the hotel in all respects is perfect. Raymond Park in which it is located, comprises seventy-five acres, and has within its borders a nine hole Golf Course, that cannot be surpassed for attractiveness of scenery, or for all the fine points that appeal to lovers of the game. The course is green throughout the winter months, and there's nothing more exhilarating than a game on its grassy slopes.

The Raymond is open from December to May, and is under the management of Gen. M. C. Wentworth, of the well-known Wentworth Hall at Jackson in the White Mountains of New Hampshire. He brings with him to the Raymond his efficient employees who have had many years of training in hotel duties under his careful supervision.

An Illustrated book of the hotel and its grounds can be had on application to The Raymond, Pasadena, California.

Views in the Grounds of The Raymond

In the 1905 Tournament of Roses supplement to the *Star News*, the full-page advertisement read, "THE FINEST LOCATED HOTEL IN THE WORLD—A PLACE FOR PARTICULAR PEOPLE. The Raymond is open from December to May, and is under the management of Gen. M. C. Wentworth, of the well-known Wentworth Hall at Jackson in the White Mountains

of New Hampshire. He brings with him to The Raymond his efficient employees who have had many years of training in hotel duties under his careful supervision." Walter Raymond took over management of the Raymond himself after 1918. Wentworth built a competing hotel in San Marino that went bankrupt shortly after opening; it later became the Huntington Hotel.

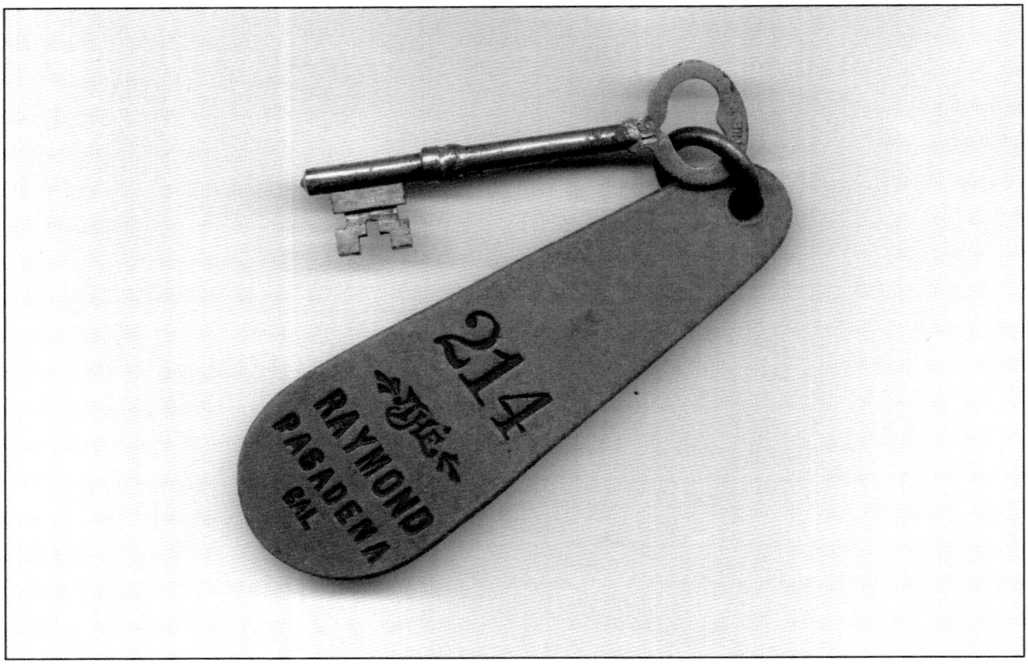

The Raymond hotel was the ultimate base camp for wealthy guests. Walter Raymond wanted his hotel to feel like their home away from home. His guests would reserve a block of rooms and remain at the hotel for the entire winter season (from a few days before Christmas to mid-April).

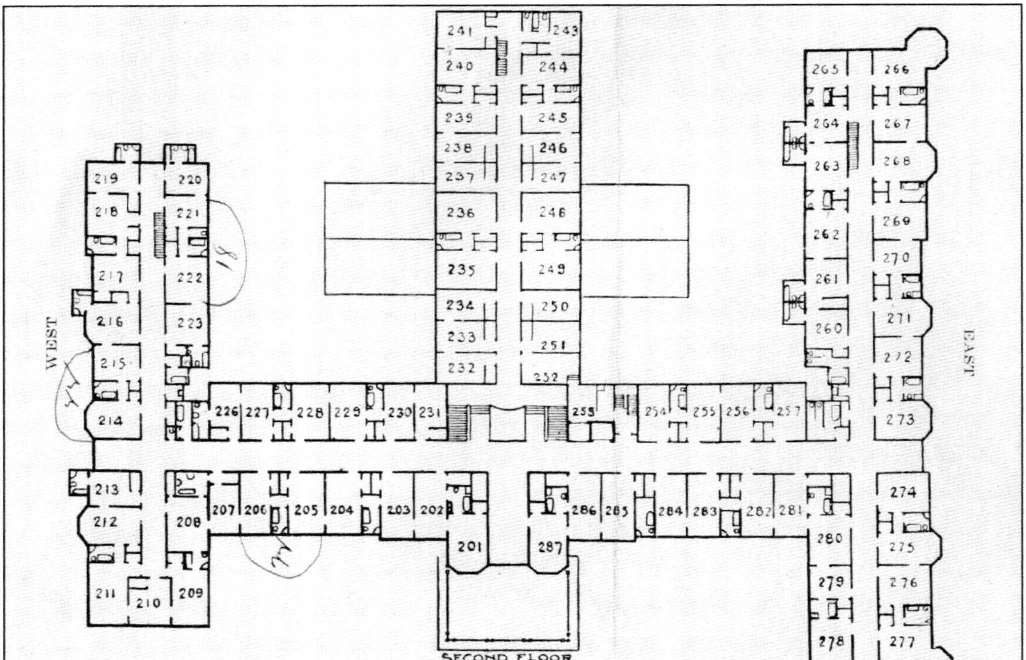

On this second-story floor plan, a hotel guest has penciled three groups of two rooms. Many of Walter Raymond's loyal guests would reserve the same groups of rooms for multiple seasons.

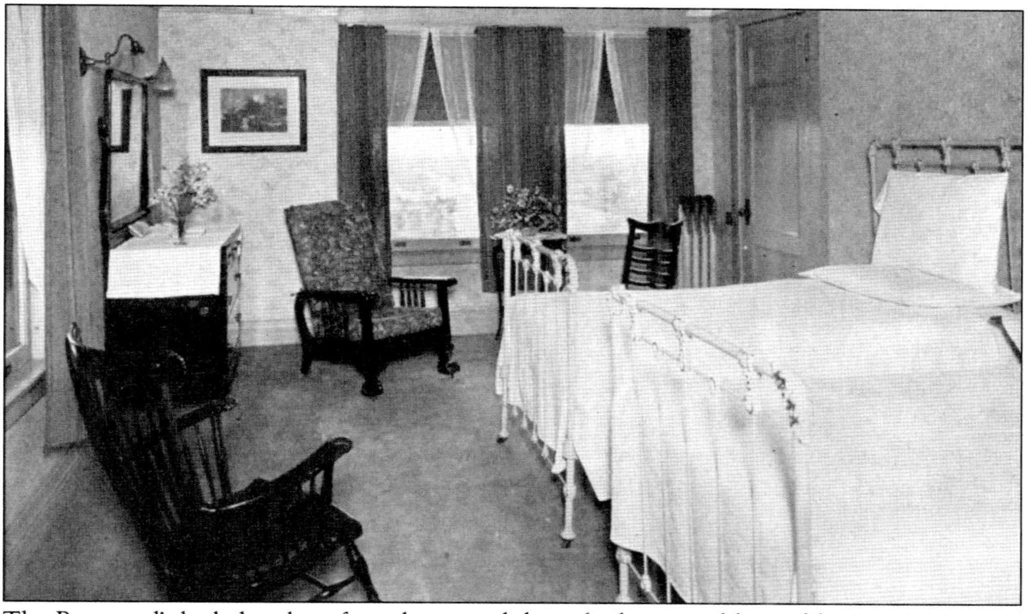

The Raymond's bed chambers furnishings and decor had a typical home-like appearance and feel. The Raymond brochure describes its bedrooms: "There is a restful charm of quiet comfort in the bedrooms, which reflect the gracious welcome Raymond guests always remember. The rooms are all large and have ample windows. Those on the south front overlook the golf course and the valley; those on the north and east look out on mountains; those on the west the rolling foothills beyond Pasadena."

This guest parlor gave guests the ability to treat parts of the hotel like their living room back home. Walter Raymond wanted each guest to feel at home in his grand hotel. He knew virtually all the guests and their families personally and was at their beck and call to address any issue that arose. To keep guests coming back season after season, Walter Raymond established a trusted loyal base of hotel patrons, which he corresponded with during the off season.

This photograph shows Walter Raymond entertaining the ladies at a grand banquet with an Asian theme. His wife, Hattie, is the woman sitting on his right (slightly behind him in the photograph). (Courtesy John Larson Collection.)

The silverware pictured here shows the partial table settings from both Raymond hotels. The spoon and knife on the left are from the second hotel (1901–1933). The spoon and cake knife on the right are from the first hotel (1886–1895).

Dinner

TOKE POINTS *on Shell*

BISQUE TOMATOES *aux Croutons* CONSOMME *Royale*
COLD BOUILLON *en Tasse*
Pulled Bread

Raymond Special Ripe Olives *Mrs. Conley's Sweet Spiced Satsumas*
Radishes *Celery*
Blanched Jordan Almonds

BOILED SALMON *Mousseline*
Sliced Cucumbers
Pommes Chateau

SWEETBREADS *Columbus*

ROAST RIBS OF BEEF *Yorkshire Pudding*
ROAST IMPERIAL VALLEY TURKEY *Cranberry Sauce*
SWEET CIDER

ARTICHOKES *Hollandaise*
BRUSSELS SPROUTS GREEN PEAS
CANDIED SWEET POTATOES MASHED POTATOES

NATIVE SQUAB BARDE, *Currant Jelly*
Saratoga Chips
ASPARAGUS *a la Russe*
DRESSED LETTUCE

ENGLISH PLUM PUDDING *Hard and Nutmeg Sauce*
LEMON MERINGUE PIE ASSORTED CAKE
MACAROONS FUDGE CAKE
CHARLOTTE RUSSE ANGEL CAKE
STRAWBERRY ICE CREAM

IMPORTED MALAGA GRAPES PERSIMMONS
DELICIOUS APPLES SLICED PEACHES *in Syrup*
APPLE SAUCE
MIXED NUTS CLUSTER RAISINS
STUFFED PRUNES LAYER FIGS

GOUDA CAMEMBERT
CHEDDER
Toasted St. Johnsbury Crackers

COFFEE

CHOCOLATE MINTS

SUNDAY, JANUARY 15, 1922

THE RAYMOND
PASADENA, CALIFORNIA

This original dinner menu from the Raymond on Sunday, January 15, 1922, shows the extensive offerings and variety of cuisine at the hotel. Imagine sitting down for dinner in the Grand Dining Hall at the Raymond and being served roast ribs of beef, Yorkshire pudding, and coffee—oh, and a couple of Raymond Special ripe olives.

This view of the Raymond defies description but speaks volumes. The sheer beauty of the South Pasadena landscape with a newly constructed hotel reborn on Raymond Hill and the mountains in the background is the main reason for its early success. Walter Raymond's claim that his hotel was the "finest located hotel in the world" was no exaggeration. (Courtesy Archives at Pasadena Museum of History.)

Jubilant guests of the Raymond return from the local groves weighed down with their haul of oranges. The orange groves were a favorite for the tourists who marveled at being able to pluck fruit from trees in the middle of winter. While staying at the hotel during the entire winter season, they would send photographs like the one at left back home to poke fun at their friends who were buried in snow.

A unique feature of the second hotel was a subway tunnel entrance located about halfway up the hill. It was built to reduce the walking distance from the waiting station on Fair Oaks Avenue to the hilltop hotel. At the end of the tunnel, an elevator carried guests up to the main lobby of the hotel. Walter Raymond boasted that it was the only one of its kind in America. The tunnel still exists on Raymond Hill today. The entrance was capped and buried during the 1940s for safety reasons.

The Raymond had a championship tennis court on the grounds that overlooked the city of South Pasadena in the distance. In this photograph, a tennis tournament draws a huge crowd, filling the stands so that the spillover spectators are forced to position their chairs on the nearby grassy hillside.

In 1902, the orange groves around the hotel gave way to a nine-hole golf course. The pavilion used before the hotel was rebuilt had now become a clubhouse.

The Raymond official golf seal—"Golf at the Raymond"—was the cover graphic for the opening-day pamphlet of the newly installed golf links during the winter of 1902.

This full-page magazine advertisement features the newly installed golf course on the hotel's park-like grounds.

At the Raymond, women were encouraged to play golf alongside men in one of the few sports of that time that allowed such play.

Helen Lengfeld first learned to play golf when she was just eight years old while her parents, Sadie and Isaac Foorman, wintered at the Raymond. The hotel had the only golf course on its own grounds in Southern California. The full-time golf professional, Willie Watson, was also available to assist guests with their game. In later years, Lengfeld organized several amateur golf tournaments for women and organized more than 400 American Women's Voluntary Services groups across America to assist the war effort during World War II. *Golf Digest* magazine named her one of the five most influential women in golf.

With installation of the golf course, one can see just how vast Walter Raymond's hotel property was in relation to South Pasadena's emerging business district along Fair Oaks Avenue. The golf course included the entire hill down to the border of present-day Garfield Park.

The Raymond's "backyard" remained the mountains, which even to this day appear as an enduring feature of all views taken on Raymond Hill. The second hotel now had a "front yard." Pictured above are the ninth-hole green (left) and the tee for the first hole (right). All the palm trees in this photograph are still on Raymond Hill—fat and slightly leaned over, but still there.

AIRSHIP BEAT AUTOMOBILE.

Race from Chutes Park to Hotel Raymond.

Aeronaut Touched Goal Two Minutes Ahead.

In 1905, Roy Knabenshue's dirigible raced a Pope-Toledo automobile from Chutes Park's baseball field in Los Angeles to the Raymond in South Pasadena. The automobile got off to a fast start. But like the story of the race between the tortoise and the hare, the automobile eventually had engine trouble, and road hazards along the Arroyo Seco caused it to fall behind. Meanwhile, Knabenshue's airborne dirigible was making steady progress toward the Raymond during the race.

Roy Knabenshue's dirigible—named the *California Arrow*—touched down on the golf course of the Raymond first, beating the Pope-Toledo by a margin of two minutes.

Roy Knabenshue in 1913 began the first passenger air service in America by taking paying customers in his dirigible on a flight 800 feet in the air over parts of the San Gabriel Valley and Los Angeles.

Roy Knabenshue built a large wooden hanger near the Raymond. Walter Raymond's son Arthur credits Roy for his lifelong passion with flight, which later led him to design such classic aircraft as the DC-3 and DC-8. (Courtesy Archives at Pasadena Museum of History.)

In this 1898 photograph, hundreds of bicycles parade down Colorado Street in a show of force to impress city planners that road improvements and more places to ride were urgently needed. Horace Dobbins (referred to as the "Grandfather of the Pasadena Freeway") began the California Cycleway Company and proposed the region's first road for bicycles from Pasadena to Los Angeles, using the Arroyo Seco as the primary route. (Courtesy Archives at Pasadena Museum of History.)

This photograph shows the tollbooth of the California Cycleway near the Green Hotel. On New Year's Day 1900, this long, elevated, wood-planked cycleway was opened to the public. One could now travel the distance between the Green Hotel and Raymond Hill nonstop by bicycle. The second-phase construction to Los Angeles via the Arroyo Seco was never built. Almost immediately after the cycleway was built, automobiles began to dominate travel on surface roads. The cycleway was later dismantled for its lumber. (Courtesy Dobbins Collection, Archives at Pasadena Museum of History.)

Vacationing motorists often stopped at orange groves to pick the fruit and pose for pictures. One tourist brochure described the experience of driving the roads on a day trip from the Raymond as "endless groves of orange trees laden with golden fruit" through "wave after wave of heavy sweet perfume."

This curious sign at the entrance road to the Raymond reads, "Automobiles are positively not allowed on these grounds." When the hotel first opened, automobiles were fast coming onto the scene. Walter Raymond forbade their presence on his hotel property because of complaints by his guests—automobiles were noisy and expelled exhaust fumes.

By the time this photograph was taken 20 years later, automobiles were fully accepted onto the hotel grounds. (Courtesy Archives at Pasadena Museum of History.)

At the top of Raymond Hill, several automobiles owned by hotel guests are parked within 100 feet of the front doors of the Raymond. Automobiles gave wealthy vacationers the ultimate freedom to travel.

Theodore Roosevelt was a well-traveled, energetic president. Soon after standing at the controls of a massive excavation crane in the Panama Canal, he made a grand tour of the Pacific Coast. On May 8, 1903, Roosevelt had lunch at the Raymond on his first stop to Pasadena after arriving in California. (Courtesy Security Pacific Bank, "History of South Pasadena" community booklet, published 1923.)

Charlie Chaplin drove out from Hollywood to have lunch with Madame Nellie Melba. According to Arthur Raymond, their lunch drew a much larger gathering of well-wishers than Roosevelt's visit.

Arthur Raymond recalled the feeling of meeting many world-famous guests at his father's hotel, describing it as quite a heady experience for a young boy. Imagine having memories of meeting Andrew Carnegie. In fact, young Arthur was seated next to him at a Sunday evening concert: "I remember joining him in the hymn singing, during which he wiped a tear from his eye." (Courtesy Library of Congress.)

On May 11, 1910, J. P. Morgan is seen striking a photographer with his cane. The Raymond offered Morgan a place of home-like comfort where he sought refuge from the ever-vigilant press. (Courtesy Library of Congress.)

On June 8, 1911, J. D. Rockefeller and his wife, Laura, are seen leaving their Pullman railcar. When Rockefeller stayed at the Raymond, he enjoyed the winter sunshine and playing golf on the hotel grounds. (Courtesy Library of Congress.)

A wealthy plumbing equipment manufacturer from Chicago, R. T. Crane lent Walter Raymond the money he needed to rebuild the hotel. Crane was a loyal guest of the Royal Raymond. Crane learned that the amount Walter received from his insurance for the loss of his first hotel by fire was not sufficient to rebuild. And just like when Walter's father stepped in to pay the amount he needed to build his hotel, it was Crane's contribution that made building the Raymond possible. (Courtesy Library of Congress.)

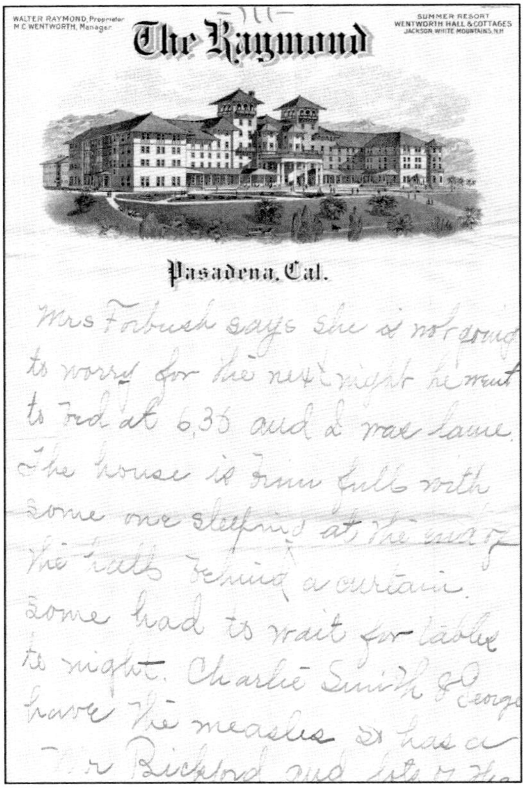

WALTER RAYMOND, Proprietor
M.C. WENTWORTH, Manager

The Raymond

SUMMER RESORT
WENTWORTH HALL & COTTAGES
JACKSON, WHITE MOUNTAINS, N.H.

Pasadena, Cal.

Mrs Forbush says she is not going to worry for the next night he went to bed at 6.35 and I was lame. The house is jam full with some one sleeping at the end of the halls behind a curtain. Some had to wait for tables to night. Charlie Smith & George have the measles & has a Mr Bickford and [illegible]

The Raymond was so popular during its first 15 years in existence that it was often overrun with guests during the peak winter season in January and February. This letter explains, "[The Raymond] is full with some sleeping at the end of the halls behind a curtain."

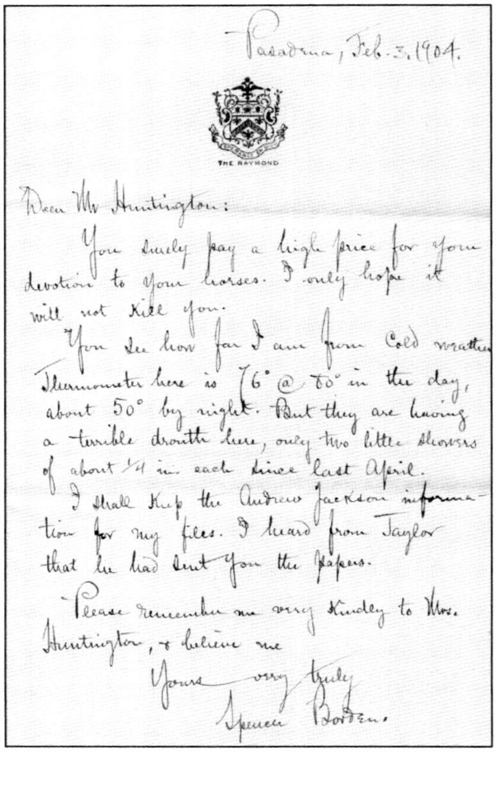

Pasadena, Feb. 3, 1904.

THE RAYMOND

Dear Mr Huntington:

You surely pay a high price for your devotion to your horses. I only hope it will not kill you.

You see how far I am from cold weather. Thermometer here is 76° @ 80° in the day, about 50° by night. But they are having a terrible drouth here, only two little showers of about 1/4 in. each since last April.

I shall keep the Andrew Jackson information for my files. I heard from Taylor that he had sent you the papers.

Please remember me very kindly to Mrs. Huntington, & believe me

Yours very truly
Spencer Borden.

This letter dated February 3, 1904, addressed to a Mr. Huntington, says, "You see how far I am from cold weather? The thermometer here is 80 degrees in the day, about 50 degrees by night. But they are having a terrible drought here, only two little showers of about ¼ inches each since April."

This beautiful flower-trimmed dinner plate with the grand hotel's image in the center was a popular souvenir for tourists visiting the San Gabriel Valley during the winter season of 1904–1905.

This masquerade party held at the Raymond hotel gives evidence the hotel guests really were a fun bunch. (Courtesy Archives at Pasadena Museum of History.)

The Adobe Flores (pictured here as it appeared in 1922) served as a tea house for hotel guests. In 1847, Mexican general Jose Flores withdrew to a camp on the nearby hilltop ("Raymond Hill") after his Californios skirmished with a U.S. Army detachment near Los Angeles. On the evening of January 9, 1847, Flores met with his advisors, which included Manuel Garfias, who owned an adobe on the Arroyo Seco in present-day South Pasadena, to draw up surrender plans to the United States, ending the Mexican Colonial period in California.

This tourist brochure promotes the charm of the historic adobe El Adobe Flores, open to the public as a tea house. The Raymond's guests frequently visited this tea house, which bordered the golf course property. The brochure reads, "Here, where guarded the dusky soldiers after the Battle of the Mesa—now come cabinet members, painters, poets, multi-millionaires, cinema stars and composers to rest under your friendly tiles and bask in the warmth of your sunlit patio."

This South Pasadena–bound Red Car served the Cawston Ostrich Farm and the Raymond, as well as commuter traffic to downtown Los Angeles. The Red Car in this photograph is crossing the Arroyo Seco at the site of the present-day York Bridge near Pasadena Avenue. (Courtesy Archives at Pasadena Museum of History.)

This incline car rests at the top of Echo Mountain to pose for a group picture. The boys just had the thrill ride of their lives, ascending nearly 3,000 feet with a 62-percent grade up the Great Incline. Thaddeus Lowe built this magnificent "railway to the clouds" to reach his resort hotels on Echo Mountain (Echo Mountain House) and Mount Lowe (Ye Alpine Tavern). The Great Incline began at the transfer point at the Rubio station; tourists would leave their electric trolley car and climb into the "white chariot" taking them up the steep incline to the top of Echo Mountain.

Another favorite mountain resort was on Mount Wilson. These guests of the Raymond appear to have put much thought into their positions around the Wilsons Peak 5,886-foot marker. The boy in the middle straddles the concrete marker like a horse. The important-looking gentleman on the right is obviously the patriarch of the family.

The Red Cars stopped at the foot of Raymond Hill at the waiting station on Fair Oaks Avenue and Columbia Street. From there, the cars traveled to downtown Los Angeles and on to all the major resort-area beaches. Pictured here is Mary Elizabeth Armour with her ukulele on the sandy beach near the Redondo Beach Bath House.

This cross-promotion brochure of the Cawston Ostrich Farm depicts the Raymond on its cover. Edwin Cawston was originally attracted to South Pasadena because of its proximity to a major resort hotel located in the same city. The Raymond brought hundreds of wealthy East Coast visitors to Cawston's doorstep during the winter months and made his new enterprise world famous.

The original Busch Gardens in the Arroyo Seco was the backyard of several mansions on Orange Grove Avenue (called "Millionaire's Row"). This view of the upper gardens contains a rustic bench and walking path with the Victorian mansion home originally built and owned by Thaddeus Lowe in the background.

These guests of the Raymond pose for a photograph in the front yard of Adolphus and Lillie Busch's winter home on Orange Grove Avenue.

Many of the guests of the Raymond liked the area so much they built homes on the nearby land that had been subdivided into fine neighborhoods. The Raymond's prominence began to fade as the hotel aged into its 30th season. The famous hotel on a hill still had a high-class reputation and was used by land developers to help promote their housing projects. The newspaper advertisement boasts, "Its location and easy accessibility, its picturesque views of the famous snow-capped mountains and gently sloping valley, the Raymond Hotel nearby; the fertile soil and wonderful health-giving climate, combined with the highest class of improvements make Oneonta Park most desirable."

Another housing development designed by architects Green and Green was Oaklawn. The high-profile housing project conceived by the famed craftsman architects was literally constructed in the shadow of the Raymond. The historic Oaklawn Bridge was built to cross over the Santa Fe Railroad tracks to Fair Oaks Avenue at the base of Raymond Hill. The stately mansion in this photograph still exists on Oaklawn today.

Margaret Mary (Loughlin) Jack was a waitress at the Raymond during the winters of 1915–1918. She is seen in this photograph, taken on the hotel grounds in 1916, wearing her "Irish Colleen" costume. Margaret was a teacher from Bennington, Vermont. In the summer months, she waited tables at the hotels at Lake Champlain. Shortly after getting to know the area from her waitress job at the Raymond, Jack decided to move to California permanently.

A variety of flowers were grown in vast fields at the foot of Raymond Hill. Flower beds made from Arroyo stone surrounded the hotel. Walkways were lined with planted flowers that bloomed during the entire winter season. Cut flowers were placed everywhere inside the hotel, making the Raymond a floral paradise like no other hotel in the world.

The Raymond's flowers were also used to decorate the hotel's annual entry in the Tournament of Roses Parade. Pictured above is Walter Raymond's 1918 float entry honoring the Red Cross for its humanitarian aid during the Great War (World War I). More than 8 million combatants and 6.6 million civilians perished during World War I. In just 20 years, an even more devastating world conflict would arise.

The Raymond property was landscaped and maintained to appeal to a guest's sense of calm and peaceful pursuit of life. The Raymond's grounds were the hotel's buffer zone that allowed the hotel to remain the home away from home guests came to know and expect season after season.

This hotel taxi carried guests from the Raymond Station up to this hilltop drop-off point in front of the hotel. This was literally the doorstep to one of Southern California's grandest hotel stories, a story about the hotel man Walter Raymond and his prominent guests, including former U.S. president Theodore Roosevelt, Charlie Chaplin, Andrew Carnegie, and others who shaped the early 20th century and in many ways helped to create the world we live in today.

Seven

A Legend Is Born

On October 3, 1934, with the hotel already closed as a result of sustained losses since the depression of 1929 and while his hotel was in the process being demolished by the bank, Walter Raymond died in his bungalow just 50 yards from the hotel's main entrance. On the hilltop today, there is evidence of the grand hotel that once stood majestically overlooking the San Gabriel Valley. First, one notices the mature palms that line the road to the hilltop. The hilltop is flat. This is the site of Raymond's dream for the last 45 years of his life.

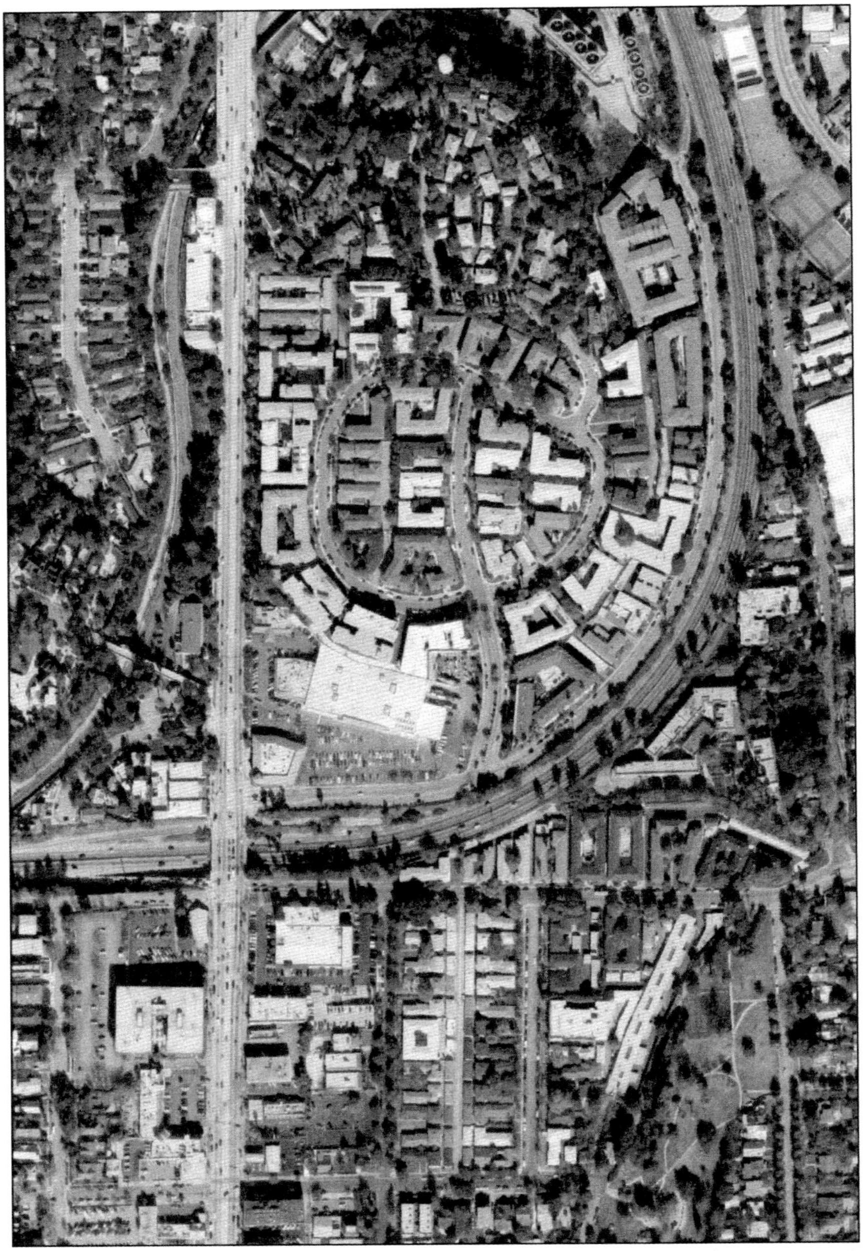

Today Raymond Hill is completely covered with construction: residential, commercial, streets, and a freeway. In this photograph, Raymond Hill is seen at the top, to the right of Fair Oaks Avenue. The curve of the Arroyo Seco Parkway around Raymond Hill cuts through where the hotel golf course used to be. Walter Raymond's hotel property extended from the hilltop all the way down to Hope Street (bottom middle) and Garfield Park (bottom right). Raymond owned 84 acres of prime real estate but never incorporated. Raymond had paid off more than $230,000 of his original loan to R. T. Crane. When Raymond could no longer make payments on the remaining $70,000 loan, now owned by a Pasadena bank, he defaulted and lost everything. The site of the hotel building is at the top of this photograph.

The author's daughter Maia gazes into the glass case at her father's Raymond Hotel collection on display at the San Marino Public Library.

This street sign is located at the flat top of Raymond Hill where the first and second hotels were built. Raymond Hill Road circles the hilltop around the boarder of where the hotel once stood. Notice in the background of this photograph one of the original palm trees, more than 100 years old, from the second hotel. (Courtesy Lauren Thomas.)

The Raymond Station is pictured here as it appeared in 1889. Other views of this Santa Fe Railroad station can be seen on page 58. (Courtesy Archives at Pasadena Museum of History.)

The Raymond Santa Fe Station survived demolition for many years and even served as a clubhouse for model railroad hobbyists during the 1930s. The station was run down in later years and was commonly used as the subject of art classes before it was eventually torn down. The photograph above was taken in the 1940s. (Courtesy John Larson Collection.)

The Raymond Hill waiting station was built in 1903 as a feature of the second hotel. Notice the distinguished gentleman in this photograph compared to the relative location of the man in the photograph below.

The Raymond Hill station was restored in 1978 and serves as a bus stop today. This location at the corner of Fair Oaks Avenue and Columbia Street has served commuters for more than 100 years. Like in a Hitchcock movie, the author has placed himself in the photograph above. (Courtesy Lauren Thomas.)

This rare photograph shows two newer features of the second hotel: the three-level observation platforms and center stairway and the large neon "Hotel Raymond" sign between the two main towers. (Courtesy Archives at Pasadena Museum of History.)

These concrete steps begin the descent down the staircase to a seat for conversation and tea in full view of the golf course grounds. (Courtesy Lauren Thomas.)

This impressive 90-year-old staircase is in perfect condition today. On either side are what would be the equivalent of special "box seats" today for comfortable viewing of the golf course lawn that stretched all the way to downtown South Pasadena at Fair Oaks Avenue and Hope Street. (Courtesy Lauren Thomas.)

This "box seat" area (there were six altogether) once had five adjustable chairs and small side tables for tea, snacks, and a good book. Notice the umbrella stand still embedded in the concrete floor after nearly 100 years. (Courtesy Lauren Thomas.)

This photograph was taken in 1907 of the main road leading up to the hotel from the Fair Oaks Avenue entrance next to the waiting station.

Today the road looks as it did more than 100 years ago. A unique feature of the second hotel was a tunnel entrance (see page 93) located about halfway up this road on an embankment below the right-side railing. The tunnel still exists on Raymond Hill today. The entrance was capped and buried during the 1940s for safety reasons. During the construction of an apartment complex in the late 1960s, the entrance was rediscovered, and the tunnel was reopened. Several renters who lived on Raymond Hill at the time walked inside the subway tunnel with a flashlight and placed notes and flowers at the end (where the elevator once carried guests up to the main hotel lobby). The tunnel was then resealed. (Courtesy Lauren Thomas.)

This original stone wall of the second hotel had a flower planter top that ran the entire length of the wall. Today it is shaded by an original pepper tree from the hotel property. (Courtesy Lauren Thomas.)

The Raymond Restaurant is a beautifully restored and maintained craftsman-style building that used to be the groundskeeper's house at the second hotel. (Courtesy Lauren Thomas.)

This wall still exists on Raymond Hill today. Stand at this exact location, glance at this photograph, and see what is there now. Focus on the photograph and then look at the wall today. That is as close as one can get to actual time travel.

Today South Pasadena's small-town charm harkens back to its early days. Still visible are the Sierra Madre (now called San Gabriel Mountains). But there are many other changes indicative of the region's rapid population growth since the late 1800s. The Historic Arroyo Seco Parkway today follows the same right-of-way the mighty steamer once did through South Pasadena. The orange groves are all gone and so too is the Raymond's golf course. And so is the sweet blossom scent that once permeated the city. What has remained is the people's indomitable spirit and sense of community. And today more than ever, they want to know about the hotel on the hill.

Walter Raymond managed a successful travel agency before becoming a hotel man. His two hotels on a hill in South Pasadena were vital to the prestige and early development of the region. Many early visitors who first came to know the area while staying at his hotel later built homes here. Walter's son Arthur went on to become vice president of the Douglas Aircraft Company, where he helped design the DC-3 and DC-8. (Courtesy South Pasadena Library.)

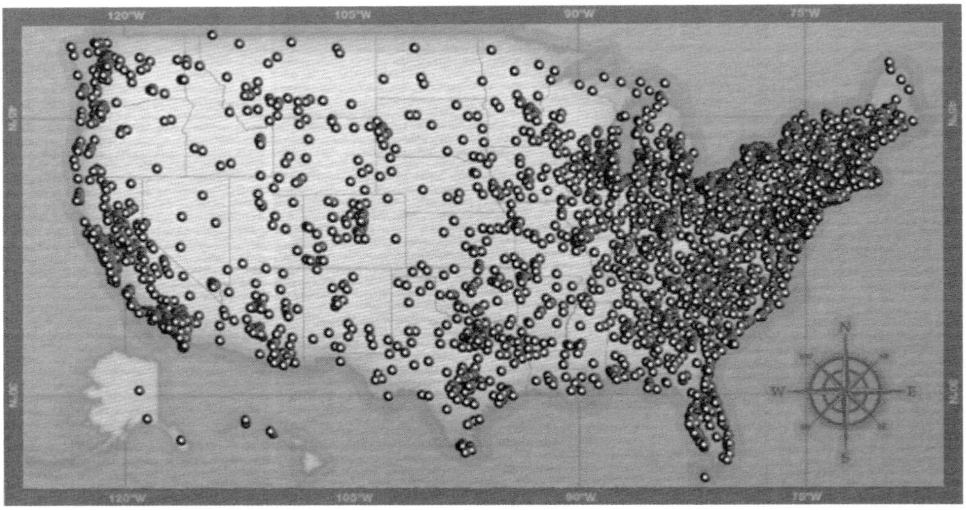

Consistent with our mission to preserve history on a local level, this book was printed in South Carolina on American-made paper and manufactured entirely in the United States. Products carrying the accredited Forest Stewardship Council (FSC) label are printed on 100 percent FSC-certified paper.

MADE IN THE USA